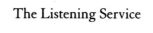

The Listening Service

The Listening Service

101 Journeys through the Musical Universe

TOM SERVICE

faber

First published in 2022
by Faber & Faber Ltd
Bloomsbury House
74–77 Great Russell Street
London WC1B 3DA

By arrangement with the BBC
The BBC logo is a trade mark of the British Broadcasting
Corporation and is used under license.

 © 2022

Typeset by Faber & Faber Ltd
Printed and bound in the UK by CPI Group (UK) Ltd, Croydon, CR0 4YY

A CIP record for this book
is available from the British Library

ISBN 978-0-571-34295-2

2 4 6 8 10 9 7 5 3 1

To BBC Radio 3's producers:
the most talented and inspirational people in radio

Contents

A COLLECTION OF INSTRUMENTS,
INNOVATIONS AND VOICES

A CORNUCOPIA OF CURIOUS IDEAS

A CONSTELLATION OF COMPOSERS AND THEIR WORKS:
WHAT THEY'VE DONE, AND HOW THEY DO IT

INTRODUCTION

Curiosity, connections and the activity of listening: an upbeat to musical adventure

The Listening Service was born of a simple contention on BBC Radio 3 in 2016: that the world of music is one of connection, not boundaries. Music is a way of navigating our place as individuals and as communities and cultures, a prism through which we can better understand and empathise with one another.

The musical impulse – to bring people together to celebrate our exquisitely evolved frequency-producing and frequency-resonating bodies, brains and spirits – is a binding thread across our humanity, geographically and historically, biologically and intellectually, from the evolution of our species to the latest science of the sounds of solar systems and black holes.

But the way the world of music is often carved up, as historians and record shops once did, and streaming services do today – dividing music into supposedly separate genres, historical periods and geographical locations – means that the potential for music to inspire and encourage a free-ranging curiosity of listening and thinking, across times, places and cultures, is often curtailed.

Yet each of us as musical humans – which is to say, every human being on earth – instinctively knows that music-making traditions are deeply connected, whatever the historians and cultural categorisers say. We know, because we feel it, that we're as likely to want to move to Donna Summer's 'I Feel Love' as we are to the last movement of Beethoven's Seventh Symphony. Those pieces share a common rhythmic intensity, an obsession with repetition, and a sense of sheer embodied abandon, whatever their differences of period and genre. They aren't connected by conventional categorisations of cultural or music-historical thinking, but they are fundamentally bound together through our visceral knowledge and experience as listeners. They both make our bodies need to move.

They certainly make mine move: and it's the attempt to restore these connections that's the real service this pro-gramme is trying to fulfil (the title, *The Listening Service*, was an unmissably fortuitous pun). Those connections aren't only across genres, they're also about harnessing music's power to make us think across whole areas of knowledge, from biology to neurology, from physics to philosophy. Above all, surfing the chain of connections that begins with our listening to and being moved by music from across humanity's history puts us in the position of imagining the world from other perspectives: from the points of view of the composers who first wrote it, the musicians who play it, and the audiences and communities and cultures who made it and make it their own.

That includes you. As well as the realisation of that spirit of connection, the other essential aim of *The Listening Service* is the restoration of our agency as listeners in the creative fab-ric of musical culture. The world – and not only the musical world – is changed by our listening.

A word on my definition of 'listening': it includes every dimension of the way our bodies are sensitised to receive sound and sound-waves, not only our hearing. Every cell of our anatomy has the potential to vibrate in sympathy with sound-waves of all frequencies, most obviously when we encounter infrasound, sounds whose frequencies are beneath human hearing but which we can't help but feel in our stomachs and through the soles of our feet – from the roar of the sea to the sub-sonic hum of the motorway and the tremors of the earth. 'Listening' also includes the way we hear sounds that no one else does in the soundtracks of our imaginations, as well as the infinitely diverse relationships we have as individuals with the audible world in the vast spectrum of differences between our hearing mechanisms.

Our world-changing powers as listeners aren't confined to the habits that are interpreted by the algorithms of so many of our interfaces with music in the digital realm of the twenty-first century. The millennia-long history of music all over the world can be told as a story of an ongoing dance between musical cultures and their audiences, in which our collective listenership drives the creativity of performers and composers, the choices they make and the sounds they produce. Without us, their audiences, musicians and composers would have no constituency. Which means that we listeners are never passive consumers of musical culture, but active participants in its creation. To listen is to be engaged, and it's to be responsible for how that culture is shaped. Whatever else our role may be in our music, whether we define ourselves as composers, performers, improvisers or singers (and the reality is that all of us are all of those things at different times of our lives), we are all listeners. We are all involved.

It's from those beliefs – in the connectedness of musical trad-itions and cultures, and in our agency and responsibility as lis-teners – that *The Listening Service* is made. And the questions, ideas, and connections of the programmes are realised through the imagination of the Radio 3 producers who magic each edition into life. It's their individual and collective virtuosity that makes audible the symbiotic links between Toots and the Maytals and Johann Sebastian Bach, Miley Cyrus and Gustav Mahler, Anna Meredith and Wolfgang Amadé Mozart.

But *The Listening Service* is also a programme that reflects the history of my own listening. That means there are often starting points, and sometimes destinations, in the 'classical music' (so-called – see chapter 52) to which my music-loving soul first migrated. But whatever the initial catalyst for your own music-immersed life, that's the just the first stepping stone in a never-ending journey of connections: in which you realise that the sighing, descending harmonies and melodies that obsessed Henry Purcell are also there in the tango of Astor Piazzolla, and they're there in the extremities of György Ligeti's music as well as in the blues of Bessie Smith. Those connections are things you can viscerally experience in the texture of the programmes, in the way we juxtapose these musics with one another. You'll be able to hear the whole half-hour-long shows by scanning the QR codes you'll find at the start of every chapter: each code takes you directly online to the relevant programme, available in perpetuity via BBC Sounds.

This book is an anthology of the show, a curated miscellany of 101 of the subjects we've covered, to stimulate your listening imagination. Each chapter introduces the catalytic idea of the episode concerned, and includes a selection of five tracks chosen from the sometimes dozens of pieces in the programme's playlist. The book is intended both as a distillation of the show and as a springboard to your own listening adventures – through the complete programmes, and beyond. Enjoy your journeys into the limitless horizons of music, and the equally infinite questions that open up, every step of the way.

OUR MUSIC AND OUR NATURE

I

Why does music move us?

Why does music move us so deeply? There's a strong statistical probability that you feel a shiver down your spine at the sheer excess of feeling that your favourite songs or symphonies create. What's going on? What is it about music that has this palpable physiological effect on us? Is it something in the music – or something in ourselves?

Either way, it's an irresistible fact of musical life. We all have particular pieces that do it for us, tracks that have an uncanny control over our nervous systems, causing our hair to stand on end, giving us goosebumps, making our breathing shallower, putting us in a state of feverish emotional stimulation – a music-induced intoxication as addictive as any narcotic.

But why? Why are these musical tingles an important feeling for us *Homo sapiens*? There seems no evolutionary advantage in being reduced to an emotionally melted wreck by a succession of sounds in the air.

The music psychologist Dr Victoria Williams has some answers. As she says, 'scientists have put people in brain scanners to see what happens when someone has a musical chill. And what we see is activation in a reward and motivation circuitry within the brain, typically a dopamine response that is associated with pleasure, so the very core part of our brain that is designed to make us do things that are rewarding can be stimulated by our favourite music.'

But whether it's because chemicals are released in the brain or because we're being wilfully manipulated by techniques like aching harmonic suspensions – when dissonant harmonies sensually linger over a resolution, something done by all the musicians and composers in the list below – so strong is the link between music and feeling, it's as if music's function is to turn sound into pure, distilled emotion.

Yet that's not really true: our bodies and brains are being worked by music, sometimes consciously, often unconsciously. But the fact that it's possible to make that kind of imaginative leap, that there's an invisible connective force between the music we hear and our emotional lives, shows just how powerful that experience has become for us all.

Why does music move us? Because it finds those parts of our feeling bodies that no other art-form can quite reach. It sounds us out, it reflects us. It gives us the shivers – and turns us all into tingle-junkies.

- ◀ Wolfgang Amadé Mozart: 'Requiem aeternam', from Requiem, K626
- ◀ Miley Cyrus: 'Wrecking Ball'
- ◀ The Carpenters: 'Goodbye to Love'
- ◀ Giovanni Battista Pergolesi: 'Stabat mater dolorosa', from *Stabat mater* in F minor
- ◀ Gustav Mahler: 'Urlicht', from Symphony no. 2, 'Resurrection'

2

Is music a universal language?

> There is as much music in the world as virtue. In a world
> of peace and love music would be the universal language,
> and men greet each other in the fields in such accents as a
> Beethoven now utters at rare intervals from a distance. All
> things obey music as they obey virtue. It is the herald of
> virtue. It is God's voice.

That was Henry David Thoreau, writing in his 1840 essay,
'The Service'. He wasn't the first, and he won't be the last, to
make the claim that music is endowed with properties that
transcend the conventions of time and space, and which can
claim to be a 'language' understood by all of the world's
peoples, in a paradise in which no one would ever again need
the services of a translating Babel fish (the brainwave-eating,
ear-dwelling piscoid that translates all the galaxy's languages
in *The Hitchhiker's Guide to the Galaxy*). We would all understand each other by communicating – in the fields, and elsewhere – through the medium of music 'in such accents as a
Beethoven now utters'.

It's proved an astonishingly seductive idea, that music might
have some innate quality that would qualify it as a culture-
connector across the globe, so that if we could only find the key

to communicating in music rather than language, we might all be understood through this language of pure unfiltered musicality, which would somehow miraculously transmit our ideas of peace and love, as per Thoreau's new musical world order, and harmonise our cultures into a music-first utopia.

We can always dream. Mind you, I don't think I'd actually like to live in music-only-land. Not least because it would be difficult to ask for a bottle of milk or a pint of beer, to discuss the price of fish, or the latest political shenanigans. Actually, I take that back: let's all communicate in music . . .

It turns out that what's really universal about the musical experience is how particular it is: the fact that we all have our own individual musical universes, of thrilling and teeming diversity and difference and cultural variety.

Is music a universal language? It's much more powerful than that: we live in a multiverse of musical possibilities, of different languages, cultures, deep structures and sonic surfaces. The miracle is that we can travel between all those musical multiverses, thanks to the fundamental connections of what it means to be musically human.

◀ Philip Glass and Ravi Shankar: 'Ragas in Minor Scale', from *Passages*
◀ Perunika Trio: 'Snoshti sum minal, kuzum Elenke'
◀ Ludwig van Beethoven: 'Heil sei dem Tag', the finale of his opera, *Fidelio*
◀ Joji Hirota and the London Taiko Drummers: 'Suisei-Hanabi'
◀ George Frideric Handel: 'Hallelujah Chorus', from *Messiah*

3

Why do babies love music?

Why are babies so sensitive to music? Our musicality is imprinted upon our tiny listening bodies even before we are born. There are biological and evolutionary reasons for this innate human predisposition to music, which raise questions about what the early development of our musically sensitive bodies tells us about our adult relationship with the music we grow to love the most. In fact, we adults have a lot to learn from the instinctive musical wisdom and receptivity of infants, from the way babies are soothed by lullabies to how they move to, and are moved by, music ranging from melodic simplicity to avant-garde energy.

Nothing gives my nieces more pleasure than out-Boulezing Boulez at the piano by hammering their hands down on the keyboard, delighting in more aggressive dissonances than many grown-ups can tolerate; and they also love getting down with one of the earworms of international babyhood, the impossibly popular and gloriously inane 'Baby Shark'. Babies and infants need this sonic sensitivity because it's vital they recognise the sounds that matter the most to them: their mother's voices, and the soundscape of the environment in which they are nurtured and cherished. In fact, babies exist in a whole world of musicking to which our adult selves will spend decades trying to return. They know – unlike us adults – that there's no separation between the world of music and the rest of their lives.

Scientists have proved the point, as Laurel Trainor from McMaster University in Canada reveals. 'The auditory system is functioning from the sixth pre-natal month. We know infants are hearing in the last trimester.' So what are the first sounds that all of our bodies respond to? 'They're in a liquid environment in the womb, so it's like hearing underwater: they get sounds from the mother, her heartbeat, her voice. And they receive sounds from the outside world – mostly low frequencies, because that's what will travel through the liquid medium.' Our soundscape in the womb is oceanic: we're in an amniotic sea of hauntingly benign sounds, vibrating hums and rumbles made by the longer wavelengths of low sounds, the soothing, muffled rhythm of our mother's heartbeat mixing with our own. This is the first soundscape that all of us know, the start of our lives as musical humans.

- ◀ Andrew Davenport: 'Tombliboo Bricks', from *In the Night Garden*
- ◀ Pinkfong: 'Baby Shark'
- ◀ Queen: 'Bohemian Rhapsody'
- ◀ Franz Schubert: Symphony no. 5 in B flat major, D485, first movement
- ◀ Imogen Heap: 'The Happy Song'

4

Music and breathing

It's something we do roughly 17,000 times a day without giving it enough thought: our breathing. In and out, a swinging pendulum of tension and release, a physical necessity when it comes to making the sounds that are most unique to all of us – our speaking and our singing. And without it there are whole families of instruments that couldn't be quickened into life: from didgeridoos to French horns, from flutes to saxophones to ophicleides.

As a physical fundamental, our breathing is also an idea, a metaphor, a way of thinking that sustains whole pieces of music: there's a breathing, a give-and-take in hour-long symphonies and box-set-long operas, just as there has to be breathing in performances by instruments that don't need the exhalation of our lungs. Violins and violinists, pianos and pianists need to breathe, too.

So how to tune into our breathing? The spirit – and the spirituality – of breathing is there in the words we use to talk about it: 'inspiration' is a divine revelation, a eureka moment, as well as being another word for our inhalation. Which means there can be no inspiration without – inspiration. 'Play a vibration in the rhythm of your breathing,' as Karlheinz Stockhausen asks his performers in 'Verbindung', in his *From the Seven Days* cycle: they make the music not by playing notes on a page, but by finding inner rhythms of breath; intuitive, instinctive, different every time. The American composer Pauline Oliveros, in her *Sonic Meditations*, is even more direct: 'Begin by taking a deep breath and letting it all the way out with air sound. Listen with your mind's ear for a tone. On the next breath using any vowel sound, sing the tone that you have silently perceived on one comfortable breath.'

Those simple instructions – taking a deep breath, listening to your breathing, becoming aware of your body and singing as you exhale – conceal a lifetime of work, whether you're a composer-guru like Oliveros or Stockhausen, or one of the vocalists whose flights of inspirational virtuosity make our own breathing bodies resonate in sympathy and astonishment. It's ironic that feats of breathing from a singer like Jessye Norman in Wagner, makes us breath-taken. Her performance of the 'Liebestod' from Wagner's *Tristan and Isolde* creates the impression of a voice that transfigures the limits of biology to fly out there, on and on, at the limits of existence, as she joins the soul of her dead lover, both 'rising higher' and 'drowning . . . in unconscious bliss', as Wagner's words say. That's a state that Jessye Norman's voice gives us through this vocal epiphany: superhuman, super-Isolde; super-normal, super-Norman.

Instrumentalists can achieve an arguably even more uncanny illusion: wind players such as oboists, saxophonists and didgeridoo players can use a technique called 'circular breathing', in which they're able to store air in their cheeks, and expel it into their instruments on their next in-breath, creating a continuous sound. It's a mind-boggling illusion that you can hear in performances from Heinz Holliger to Kenny G (who holds the world record for the longest single circular-breathed note, more than forty-five minutes) to William Barton.

But it's not only these outer edges of the possible in breathing that are important to music. As physical reality and as metaphor for the give-and-take of the structures of whole performances and entire pieces, breathing makes our music human. As another of Pauline Oliveros's *Sonic Meditations* suggests: breathe, and fly, and breathe, and fly . . .

◀ Nicola Porpora: 'Vaghi amore, grazie amate', from *La festa d'Imeneo* (Cecilia Bartoli, Il Giardino Armonico)
◀ Cornelius Cardew: 'Paragraph 7', from *The Great Learning*
◀ Richard Wagner: 'Liebestod', from *Tristan and Isolde* (Jessye Norman, Vienna Philharmonic, Herbert von Karajan)
◀ Brian Ferneyhough: *Unity Capsule* for solo flute
◀ William Barton: *Didgeridoo Solo no. 2*

5

Is birdsong music?

Is birdsong music? It's one of the most complex but calming sounds that we encounter. Charles Darwin thought birdsong answered the same biological needs as human music. Both were fundamentally about the necessity of attracting a mate, and the quasi-linguistic significance of birdsong made it a distant ancestor of human language. But is what we hear as bird-'song' anything like our 'music' for the four thousand species of singing birds? Are birds really communicating through their calls and avian virtuosities the same way we do when we speak? What sounds like sheerly, songfully beautiful sound to us when we hear a goldcrest or skylark may mean something completely different: 'Move! Here comes a marauding hawk!', if you're a thrush or chaffinch; or 'I've found some juicy earthworms!', if you're a parenting robin or blue-tit.

What we can at least say is how human composers have been inspired by the sounds of birdsong over the millennia. It starts with a cuckoo in a song that was first written down in the thirteenth century, 'Sumer is icumen in'; another cuckoo chirps throughout Louis-Claude Daquin's 1735 keyboard piece 'Le coucou', a later relative peers over a calm pool in Beethoven's brook in the slow movement of his 'Pastoral' Symphony, in 1808.

And that's just a cuckoo through the centuries: but the most famous – and famously prodigious – compositional birder is the twentieth-century French composer Olivier Messiaen. Messiaen found in birds both musical and spiritual inspiration. Notating birdsong was a ready-made musical resource for the composer when he faced a creative impasse, but birds were also tokens of God's grace and love. His birds teem throughout his music from the 1950s onwards: they're emissaries of mercy on the grandest scale in his opera, *St Francis of Assisi*, they sing and soar through the orchestral textures of *Chronochromie*, and they're brilliantly, vibrantly heard in his piece for piano and ensemble, *Oiseaux exotiques*.

And yet, the truth is that what Messiaen writes down bears only a passing resemblance to the sounds that birds actually make. Birdsong is simply too fast, and too high, to be accurately transcribed in music, and it uses notes of the scale that just don't exist on Messiaen's piano. It's a song that operates to a different scale of time and meaning from any humanly produced system of sounds, whether we're talking about music or language.

So birdsong clearly, definitively, isn't music in the sense that we understand it, in the way that birds use their songs and calls themselves. But for us humans, it's a different story. Birdsong really is music for us: every time we whistle the call of the cuckoo, or the starling, or the blackbird; and when composers use birdsong as musical material, it's alchemised into the realm of human music – in a Messiaen piano piece, in Einojuhani Rautavaara's *Cantus Arcticus*, or Ottorino Respighi's *Pines of Rome*.

And in Jonathan Harvey's *Bird Concerto with Pianosong*, for chamber orchestra, electronics, and solo piano, composed in 2001. As Harvey says, '"Real" birdsong [is] stretched seamlessly all the way to human proportions – resulting in giant birds – so that a contact between worlds is made.' Your imagination and your whole being seem to take flight when you hear this music, as you're transported into another dimension of feeling through its sheer beauty, feeling what it might be like to be 'human in the mind of a bird'.

◀ 'Sumer is icumen in'
◀ Olivier Messiaen: 'Epode', from *Chronochromie*
◀ Richard Blackford and Bernie Krause: *The Great Animal Orchestra*
◀ Jonathan Harvey: *Bird Concerto with Pianosong*
◀ Ottorino Respighi: 'The Pines of the Janiculum', from *Pines of Rome*

6

Sound of the underground

What happens when we dare to listen to the music and sounds of underground regions of our world and our imagination – if we delve through earth and into cave, through stone and into fire? How have composers sung their songs of the earth? And what's the relationship between how composers have made the earth resonate in their creative worlds and what the earth and its subterranean regions actually sound like?

One of the most dramatic pieces in which a composer has tried directly to realise the impact of seismic subterranea is the tone-poem *Hekla*, by the Icelandic composer Jón Leifs. It's a musicalisation of a volcanic eruption: Leifs saw Hekla's eruption in 1947, the biggest of the century in Iceland, and his music creates one of the most gigantically ambitious musical onomatopoeias ever conceived. Hekla's violence is remade with anvils, ship's chains, sirens, rocks – the earth literally turned into an instrument – church bells, canon, shotguns – along with a huge orchestra and choir. Leifs uses massive pile-ups of dissonance, and creates a rhythmic power that's relentless: when you experience this piece, you have the certain feeling of humanity's tremulous tininess in the face of the furnace of the earth.

Dissonance, noise, a combination of churning industry and hellscapes of fire and rock: Jón Leifs isn't alone in his compositional imagination. Richard Wagner, in his music for the dwarves' realm of Nibelheim in the *Ring* cycle, and Howard Shore's score for the orcs of Isengard in Peter Jackson's *Lord of the Rings* conjure similarly sulphurous soundworlds.

But what songs does the underground realm really sing, what microphones can hear down there in the seismic sound-scape of the earth, unfiltered by orchestra, movie studio or opera house? Jez riley French is a composer and sound re-cordist who has captured the sounds of Icelandic volcanic fumaroles, whose high-pressure steam makes them sound like cosmic kettles of creation: alarming, violent sounds that can't be tamed by human imagination. Jez's geophones have heard even deeper than those fumaroles, and listened to the rotation of the earth. Our world makes an infrasonic vibra-tion – sound vibrating at frequencies beneath the range of our human ears, which we feel rather than hear.

And yet in our music about the earth there are deep truths to be heard, even if they don't sound anything like the sounds of the spinning earth, its volcanoes, fumaroles, or tectonics. In the achingly long leave-taking of the final movement from Gustav Mahler's *Das Lied von der Erde*, his 'Song of the Earth', the words 'ewig, ewig' – 'forever, forever' – are stretched by the singer into the endless blue distance; so slowly that Mahler's music seems to dissolve time. Everything stops in the embrace of the earth – as it must for all of us. Underground, where gods and monsters live; the energy of where we all come from, and where we'll all return.

- Jón Leifs: *Hekla*
- John Luther Adams: *Earth and the Great Weather*
- Howard Shore: 'A Knife in the Dark', from the score for *The Fellowship of the Ring*
- Björk: 'Mutual Core', from *Biophilia*
- Gustav Mahler: *Das Lied von der Erde*

7

The sea

If you put a conch-shell to your ears, you don't hear the sea: you hear the micro-acoustic of the whorls of the shell, and the amplification of environmental sound around you. But as Dante Gabriel Rossetti puts it, we want to imagine that we are hearing, 'The same desire and mystery / The echo of the whole sea's speech.' Why are we, as humans, so seduced by the sea's siren songs? And why have composers so often used the sea's sublime sonic reality as the inspiration for their music?

I think it's because there is a sensual and symbiotic connection between the physicalities of both music and the sea. We feel a total immersion in sound as we do in no other art-form, and we lose ourselves out there on the waves, when we dive and swim, or when our eyes look out over the apparent infinity of the ocean.

So how do you create in sound the sense of being overwhelmed that we feel when we're confronted by the sublimity of the ocean? Claude Debussy's *La Mer* is an awesome, thrilling, and dazzling ocean of sound and motion for orchestra. A few years later, in 1914, Jean Sibelius wrote his tone-poem *The Oceanides*, which creates a tsunami of musical momentum that crests in an irresistible and frightening climax, as its waves of energy peak in phase with one another.

Much later in the twentieth century, there's a four-minute work for orchestra called *Sea-Change* by the Greek composer Iannis Xenakis, who used to take his kayak out into the teeth of a stormy sea in Corsica, and knew the power of the sea at first hand. Xenakis's piece is an uncompromising shard of sublime orchestral sonority: the visceral thrills of the glissandos in the strings make you feel you're on the top of a wave in a tiny boat before your stomach drops and you plunge down the other side. It's as unpredictable and as powerful as a sudden tempest.

But in 2013, the American composer John Luther Adams created a forty-five-minute piece that's the closest thing we have to music that is both a transliteration of the physical motions of our seas into musical forms, and a creative transcendence of them. *Become Ocean* is radically objective: it swells and surges into gigantic billowings of orchestral sonority and saturated harmony, and then subsides into Sargasso-like moments of stasis. It moves according to its own laws that seem to be independent of human ideas like structure and time and story.

And yet John Luther Adams's music has a sublime, cathartic power over us. And that power has a point – and a truly transformative one. As John Luther Adams says: 'Life on this earth first emerged from the sea. And as the polar ice melts and the sea level rises, we humans find ourselves facing the prospect that once again we may quite literally become ocean.' *Become Ocean* returns us to a fundamental connection between the immersive experiences of listening and the sea: our listening is an ocean – we just have to dive into it.

- Claude Debussy: 'Sirènes', from *Nocturnes*
- Groove Armada: 'At the River'
- Iannis Xenakis: *Sea-Change*
- Radiohead: 'Weird Fishes/Arpeggi', from *In Rainbows*
- John Luther Adams: *Become Ocean*

8

In space no one can hear you sing . . .

As the posters for Ridley Scott's *Alien* said in 1979: 'In space, no one can hear you scream'. And Ridley was right, because no one could hear you scream, sing, or make any other loud noise in the empty wastes of our ever-expanding universe. Although it's not quite a vacuum, the molecules of gas are simply too widely spaced to allow sound-waves to pass through the medium of the interstellar regions. All those millions of hours of sci-fi soundtracks and sound effects that are part of the way that we imagine what happens out there in the cosmos: they're all – surprise, surprise! – physics-bending fictions. You really can't and will never be able to hear a laser in space, despite George Lucas's best attempts to convince us otherwise.

Despite this silence of the void, why do human musicians and composers want to make music about space? There are some common features of space-obsessed music, like the Danish composer Rued Langgaard's *Music of the Spheres*, and Gustav Holst's *The Planets*. Langgaard's apocalyptic vision is conjured by very high and very low sounds: he creates a sense of emptiness between the double basses and low brass at the bottom of the texture, and twinkling, celestial flutes and other high woodwind above. There is a literal sense of orchestral space in this music, so that our feet are on the earth of the droning lower instruments while our imaginations soar above them in the sounds of those higher, star-travelling instruments.

And Gustav Holst does something similar, in music written at around the same time, during and just after the cataclysm of the First World War, in the final movement from *The Planets*, 'Neptune'. Holst uses the ethereal wordless voices of an off-stage female choir, as well as creating awesome serenity in the upper strings. In its slowness and its harmonies unmoored from conventional forces of tonality, Holst creates a cosmic wonder in music that's flung into a gravity-less region of musical time and space.

Later in the twentieth century, the Hungarian composer György Ligeti's *Atmosphères*, from 1961, wasn't originally inspired by outer space at all, yet it's become the sound of the deep cosmic beyond, thanks to Stanley Kubrick's use of it in his film *2001 – A Space Odyssey*. Ligeti uses orchestral extremes of high and low, but he goes further than Holst or Langgaard, turning the piece into a simultaneously atomic and galactic investigation of new worlds of sound: musical matter collides and coalesces and explodes in front of your ears. *Atmosphères* is a nine-minute engine of celestial creation and destruction in orchestral sound.

Those are just a handful of the sounds about space; there are so many more: from Joseph Haydn's *Creation* to David Bowie's 'Space Oddity', from Bebe and Louis Barron's music for the movie *Forbidden Planet* to Delia Derbyshire's conjuring of the *Doctor Who* theme tune. The sounds of space are as dizzyingly various and cosmically adventurous as the composers who have imagined them. And thanks to NASA's sonifications, we can even hear sounds made from the electromagnetic energy of deep space itself: weird and wonderful whistlings and whoopings, the actual music of the spheres.

Thanks to all of these human- and science-made sounds of space, the world of music is its own cosmos that we terrestrial space-dwellers can teleport ourselves across.

- ◀ John Williams: 'The Imperial March', from the soundtrack for *The Empire Strikes Back*
- ◀ Elton John: 'Rocket Man'
- ◀ Bebe and Louis Barron: 'Overture', from the soundtrack for *Forbidden Planet*
- ◀ Terry Riley: 'One Earth, One People, One Love', from *Sun Rings*
- ◀ Eric Idle: 'The Galaxy Song'

9

The music of the night

What happens when composers and songwriters have listened to the sounds of the night? What have they heard in the dark? The night has inspired composers – paradoxically – to some of their most radiantly unforgettable creations, on epic and intimate scales, from Wagner's *Tristan and Isolde* to Debussy's orchestral *Nocturnes*; from the Bee Gees to Eurythmics. So what's the connection between our nocturnal lives and the soundworlds composers, producers and singers have made when they hymn the sounds of the night?

It all comes from the circadian rhythms that regulate our lives as *Homo sapiens*. We are creatures – most of us anyway – who are most active during the day, so the night is a place in which our consciousness wanders along paths of wonder and fantasy, in which our desires and fears are given free rein in dream as twilight fades to black and sleep claims us. That's what Johannes Brahms makes happen in his 'Lullaby', music of lulling repetitions, in a slow tempo, and a soft dynamic, whose melodic simplicity compels us to sleep in just a few minutes.

In the twenty-first century, Max Richter does something similar on the scale of eight hours: writing *Sleep*, the longest continuous composition that has ever been broadcast on Radio 3. Richter's music inhabits a strange somnolent interzone in which the music is there both to be listened to with your conscious mind – and attended to by the powers of your unconscious when you fall asleep. It's music both to calm the attention, and, to command it. It's made of soft-focused chords, ambient drones and a very slow tempo, but its patterns don't simply repeat for eight hours. Instead, the music billows and flows as your breathing and your brainwaves do when you sleep, a musical mirror of our sleep patterns.

But that's only one side of what night-music can be. After all, it's not only sleeping that we humans get up to at night. We also like to party, and composers have been our catalysts for nocturnal bacchanals, whether in the Vienna of the 1780s, in the serenades that composers like Mozart composed for out-door entertainment, or 1970s New York, as disco consumed the clubs, the city, and the world.

We dance, and we dream, and in their dreams, composers have found musical inspiration, from Giuseppe Tartini's nightmare of the Devil appearing in his bedroom, a vision that inspired his 'Devil's Trill' sonata, to Paul McCartney's 'Yester-day', to Igor Stravinsky's Octet.

Because music – all music – is as fantastical and as evanes-cent as our dreams. And yet, unlike our dreams, music is a tangible reality, too, of sound-waves, and notes and rhythms, and frequencies that vibrate into our bodies. What's the con-nection between music and the night? From serenades to sur-real visions, our rhythms of the night won't stop reverberating: dancing, dreaming, sounding out our subconscious. Music is a collective waking dream.

- ◀ Max Richter: *Sleep*
- ◀ Eurythmics: 'Sweet Dreams'
- ◀ Arnold Schoenberg: *Erwartung*
- ◀ Richard Wagner: *Tristan and Isolde*, Act 2
- ◀ Bee Gees: 'Night Fever', from the soundtrack to *Saturday Night Fever*

10

The magical forest of Romanticism

The forests of Europe have been the crucible of so many composers' imaginations. In the nineteenth century, the wildwood, as idea and reality, gave rise to an entire artistic movement in the sounds of German Romanticism. But where does the idea of the forest as incubator of our deepest and darkest fears and joys begin? Our human ancestors lived in ancient forests, knowing them as places of plenty as well as fearful predation. They surely sang songs of their journeys into the forest when they returned to their caves, playing bone-flutes and creating rituals to ask this Ur-forest to provide them with life, food and shelter; or they lamented their dead, lost to the beasts, on the hunt.

That early history of humanity living as part of the forest changes by the time we get to Vienna in the early nineteenth century – to jump wildly through forested history. By that time, with the movement of the centres of population to cities, the forest re-emerges in our cultural imaginations as a place of sublime fear and exalted escapism. As we become more 'civilised', so the forest – wild, untamed, a place that seethes with animal fears and where we can express our primal passions away from the bright lights of society – emerges from the depths of our unconscious.

That's what so many of the soundworlds of nineteenth--century Romanticism are about, from Schubert's songs, like his tone-poem of forest feeling, 'Im Walde', to Schumann's piano music, to Mendelssohn's fairy-tales. But it's Carl Maria von Weber's operas, and specifically the 'Wolf's Glen' scene from Act 2 of *Der Freischütz*, composed in 1821, that really consecrates these ideas. Weber's music turns the forest into a community of supernatural beings, and of dark and daemonic magic. He creates a combination of lowering harmonies, dazzlingly dark orchestration, and even uses a wailing, screeching choir to conjure up flashes of lightning from the cauldron, ghouls and skeletons flying through the air on horseback, as Caspar invokes Samiel, the Black Huntsman. This scene is the solar plexus of the idea of the forest as a place of the sonic sublime. No 'Wolf's Glen' scene: no Wagner, not much Berlioz, not a lot of Mahler and Liszt: it's music whose unbounded adventure through a dark fairy-tale forest is still shocking today.

And yet, still more surprising are the sounds that the forest itself makes. The composer and sound recordist Jez riley French has revealed that instead of a bucolic relaxation of dawn choruses and lovely copses of trees swaying in the winsome wind, the British forest is a place of infra-sonic violence and ultra-sonic cries and screeches, in the brutal competition for survival that every forest-scape conceals.

Forest are places in which we go to the limits of our civilisation and our imagination. The music we make about them is the sound of our fears and our hopes – and can even be a prophecy of our future. Jean Sibelius's tone-poem *Tapiola* is a forest-inspired musical revelation of the inhuman forces of the forest: their true darkness is blacker and more desperate than any fairy-tale can summon, than any psychodrama can conjure. It's music that's a prophecy of what happens when we have so destroyed our environment that we consign ourselves to our own oblivion, and the forces of nature – impassive, inviolable, inevitable – take over.

- ◀ Carl Maria von Weber: 'Wolf's Glen' scene, from *Der Freischütz*, Act 2
- ◀ Richard Wagner: 'Forest Murmurs', from *Siegfried*
- ◀ Jean Sibelius: *Tapiola*
- ◀ Jez riley French: *Tree, Northumbria*
- ◀ Arnold Schoenberg: *Erwartung*

11

The power of love songs

What is the power of the love song? Why are we so addicted to love? The very earliest writing in the historical record, by the priestess Enheduanna from the Sumerian city of Ur, in the twenty-third century BC, are words of love poetry that would almost certainly have been sung. And from the troubadours and the troubairitzes of the turn of the first millennium in Europe, to the songs of Franz Schubert and the operas of Giacomo Puccini in the nineteenth and twentieth centuries, to the songs of Elton John and Donna Summer, love and lust are essential catalysts for our music.

And the story of our love music isn't just a story of how songs, symphonies and operas have expressed the richest and most exquisite and exposing of human experiences. It's also a story of how the power of love music has changed our societies: how admitting these feelings in music has started journeys of social and cultural evolution, and has opened up new ways of relating to each other as individuals and communities. Our love music charts a story of human and emotional change that goes on, and which will never stop.

The world's most popular opera is Verdi's *La traviata*, from 1853: a tragically powerful embodiment of the darker stories of love. The romance between Alfredo and Violetta, a courtesan, is hardly the kind of story that gives love – or the society that crushes it – a good name. The story is based on Alexandre Dumas *fils's La Dame aux camélias*, and *La traviata*, 'The Fallen Woman', is a tragedy in which love doesn't only fail to triumph, but is squashed by a poisonous confection of disease, social opprobrium, tendentious moralising and misogynist paranoia ultimately leading to Violetta's death.

It's a drama that's messy, that's realistic, that's thwarted and thrawn, and whose every bar resounds with emotional and dramatic connection with its audiences. Verdi uses the popular tunes of the time, the waltzes and polkas that were Europe's contemporary soundtrack of dissolute pleasure, to dramatise Violetta's life of desperate partying in the first act – a sign of how cutting and coruscating he wanted the work's social critique to be. And he gives Violetta music of heartrending simplicity in the aria 'Addio, del passato', when she is at her rawest, her lowest, and her most shockingly ill, in Act 3.

The way we sing out stories about love is as revealing of the social and cultural fissures of our communities as it is emotionally cathartic for all of us as individuals. And our entire human impulse to make music, to be musical, is a direct result of our need to express our love for each other: whether that's our deepest physical desires and emotional needs, or the way we communicate a sacred love for a divine presence. Without that symbiosis of love and music, our lives would be much quieter, a whole lot less emotional, less cathartically tragic – and infinitely less fun.

◀ Robert Palmer: 'Addicted to Love', from *Riptide*
◀ Britney Spears: 'Toxic', from *In the Zone*
◀ Franz Schubert: 'Ständchen', from *Schwanengesang*
◀ Bessie Smith: 'Empty Bed Blues'
◀ Giuseppe Verdi: *La traviata*

12

Can music scare us?

Fear: how can music make us jump out of our seats, bring us out in a cold sweat of terror, and conjure up demons, ghosts, ghouls, and all the denizens of the darkness?

A monster mash-up of a scary musical history of the ways that composers have created pieces that go bump in the night over the last four hundred years might start with the seventeenth-century composer Marin Marais on the operating table, with 'The Bladder-Stone Operation', music that describes an operation to remove a urinary bladder calculus – then a terrifyingly dangerous procedure – complete with the horror of the patient in the screams and scrapes of the viola da gamba.

In the mid-twentieth century, Benjamin Britten's operatic ghost story *The Turn of the Screw* curdles innocence into evil, nowhere more so than in the creepy nursery-rhyme that Miles sings. Performed by a boy treble, this music is warped by Britten into something terrible and strange; elsewhere, the bell-sounds of the celeste chime for the ghostly corruption of the spectral tenor, Peter Quint. And in the twenty-first century, there's Mica Levi's soundtrack of uncanny sonic slippage for the film *Under the Skin*, made from warped instrumental sounds and liquefying electronics for the subtle but savage body horror of the movie.

And it's cinema where we so often encounter our darkest fears made visible, and audible. John Carpenter is a director and composer whose films and music have been scaring the subconsciouses of audiences for forty years and more. In *Halloween*, Michael Myers – the baseball-cap-wearing masked killer who terrorises Jamie Lee Curtis's character and who just won't die – stalks the movie even when he's not on screen, thanks to Carpenter's lo-fi synth soundtrack. The space Carpenter leaves between high and low in his music opens up a horrifying void for us to populate with our imaginations, and with its trippy 5/4 loop – five uncanny beats to the bar – the Myers theme can be repeated over and over, or stopped suddenly for a breathtaking silence, only to be interrupted by one of the film's perfectly timed jump-scares.

Whether it's Carpenter's soundtracks, or the diabolical visions of Wolfgang Amadé Mozart's *Don Giovanni*, Hector Berlioz's *Symphonie fantastique* or Alfred Schnittke's *Faust Cantata*, we need the cathartic experience of the occasional musical hell-ride now and then. How else can we appreciate the musical light without the dark? Music takes us to a place called fear through its sinister machinations, its ghostly apparitions, its cinematic associations, and its own stories quicker than anything else I know. Those sounds are inside us all too, in our dreams, in the corner of our hearing, in those places just beyond our conscious senses; the noises we try to block out – but which we can't escape. Enjoy. If you dare . . .

◀ György Ligeti: 'Kyrie', from Requiem
◀ John Carpenter: soundtrack for *Halloween*
◀ Alfred Schnittke: 'Es geschah', from *Faust Cantata*
◀ Giuseppe Verdi: 'Dies irae', from Requiem
◀ James Bernard: soundtrack for *The Horror of Dracula*

13

Music for mourning

All over the world, music is an essential part of mourning. It's as if the substantial insubstantiality of music – indelibly there, present in the air, as a physical vibration in our bodies, and then suddenly gone, disappearing, fading, echoing – is a metaphor for the way our own lives come into existence, bloom, and fade. Music for a funeral, or music that we use to conjure the memory of a loved one, is a magical presence that can carry a spirit to whatever vision of the beyond is part of the belief system of our culture.

The sounds of this funerary music are as diverse as the traditions across the world that commemorate and carry the dead. In the West, our funerary music is often minor-key, slow, and stentorian, like the funeral marches of Beethoven or Chopin; or it's lamenting and consolatory, in music that's become associated with public mourning, whatever the composer's intention, like Barber's *Adagio for Strings*.

Originally part of a string quartet written in 1936, Barber's *Adagio* has become a vessel for national grief and trauma, marking Presidential deaths from Franklin D. Roosevelt to John F. Kennedy, the funerals of public figures like Albert Einstein, and the commemoration in London's Trafalgar Square of the victims of the 2015 Charlie Hebdo attack in Paris. The director

Oliver Stone's use of Barber's music at the end of his Vietnam-protesting movie *Platoon* is another example of how this music has become synonymous with a lament for the dead. It's so powerful because Barber's music is made of aching passing dissonances, and these slow-moving, slow-resolving harmonies are musical wounds that resonate as carriers of our own emotion. The music sounds what we can't say. Listening to it in a state of grief is a way of exorcising and salving our trauma.

Yet funerary music isn't always slow and keening – just as it isn't in the most popular songs that are chosen for funerals in the UK, from Monty Python to Frank Sinatra. In New Orleans's traditions, the musical rite of passage moves from dirges and hymns that cut the body loose, through spirituals that swing, towards joyously powerful dance music, in a flamboyant, cathartic celebration of the lost life. And in the Famadihana tradition of the Malagasy people of Madagascar, relatives are disinterred every few years from their graves. The bodies are wrapped in new clothes and the community dances with them to deliriously ecstatic music, before returning them to their tombs, renewing the bonds with their ancestors, revelling in memories of their lives.

For all their differences, all these musics and traditions are part of how music expresses and mediates our griefs. Music is a sounding arc of connection that takes the dead – and us, the living – across the threshold, through the veil.

◀ Henry Purcell: *Music for the Funeral of Queen Mary*
◀ Johann Sebastian Bach: Chaconne, from Partita no. 2 in D minor for solo violin, BWV 1004
◀ Gustav Mahler: Adagietto, from Symphony no. 5
◀ John Tavener: *Song for Athene*
◀ Frank Sinatra: 'My Way'

14

Anger in music

It doesn't take much to make us angry, does it? The injustices and inequalities of the world: when you lose your glasses for the fourteenth time this morning; when your politics and democracy are a shade on the dysfunctional side; or when your internet service provider puts you on hold for just another few minutes . . . . If only we had some music to exorcise our angry demons of love and jealousy, of daily vexation and annoyance, of political protest and petty aggression.

Thankfully, music has been doing just that for centuries, representing the fire of political protest and the passions unleashed when love goes wrong, in music by Bob Dylan or the punk rage of 999. You want revenge? You got it: listen to the Queen of the Night's arias from Mozart's *Magic Flute*, or to heavy metal bands such as Disturbed or Slayer, with their screams and shouts and visceral power.

What techniques are composers and musicians using when they turn their righteous indignation and love-torn jealousy and rage into a creative fire for their music? Think about what happens to us when we erupt in rage: it's often shouty, noisy, volcanically spectacular – and it doesn't last very long. That's exactly what composers have done when they want to portray tempestuous rage: the shorthand for anger is to compose short sharp shocks of violence, speed and pounding rhythms, usually in a minor key – and, if you were writing an opera in the 1720s, a spot of demonically virtuosic vocalising.

That's what George Frideric Handel makes happen in his opera *Julius Caesar*. In the aria 'Empio, dirò, tu sei', Caesar is uncontrollably cross with Tolomeo, because Tolomeo has just executed Pompey, despite Caesar having just pardoned him. Presented with Pompey's head, Caesar loses it, incandescent at Tolomeo's cruelty, in a fabulous eruption of musical rage. Handel writes strings striking down like daggers in the introduction, the sound of minor-key pent-up fury. And when we hear the voice, Handel's themes spit the words out, terrifyingly loudly: 'Unholy monster, get out of my sight, you are the image of cruelty!' It's the sound of a violent put-down, and the music moves the way you would land a physical blow, an undodgeable punch. Caesar's anger boils even more forcefully over the word 'crudeltà', 'cruelty': Handel writes a melisma – lots of notes on one syllable – which is often a sensual, beautiful effect. But not in this aria. At this speed, it's the sound of an intensifying storm of rage.

Those markers of anger that were established by Handel and many other eighteenth-century operatic composers in their rage arias – fast tempo, minor key, vertiginous rises and falls of the melody, explosive fortissimo virtuosity – define what anger sounds like in music of subsequent centuries, from Berlioz to Britten, Beethoven to Wagner. In fact, the musical lexicon of anger is among the most consistent representations of emotion in music that we have, over the ages and across the genres, from the Days of Wrath unleashed by Verdi and Dvořák in the 'Dies Irae' movements of their Requiems, to heavy metal shredding and the fury of political protest songs.

41

The secret, and the paradox, is that angry music doesn't amplify our own anger. It thrills us – and even makes us feel better. Angry music exorcises our vexatious demons. To go through these emotions in this music is to redeem and expiate them. It's true catharsis: angry music is among the most therapeutic and the most consoling that we have. Get angry, feel better!

◀ George Frideric Handel: 'Empio, dirò, tu sei', from *Julius Caesar*
◀ Disturbed: 'Down With The Sickness', from *The Sickness*
◀ The Commander-In-Chief (Berit Hagen): 'Why So Hostile?'
◀ Ludwig van Beethoven: Symphony no. 6 in F major, op. 68, 'Pastoral', fourth and fifth movements
◀ Bob Dylan: 'Idiot Wind', from *Blood on the Tracks*

A MISCELLANY OF MUSICAL
FUNDAMENTALS

15

Silence!

The place where all musical performances begin, and where they must all end; the state out of which we are born, but to which we, too, must return: silence.

And yet: as the American composer John Cage said, there is 'no such thing as silence'. Cage knew that was true after he experienced one of the quietest man-made spaces on earth in 1951: the anechoic chamber at Harvard University. These chambers are full of specially designed foam insulators that muffle sounds of every frequency, so there is no echo. It's an uncanny experience, in which you can see a bigger space, but you can't sense it with the echolocation of your voice and your hearing. Acoustic space seems to shrink, Alice-like, to the size of your body – even though there is a larger volume around you.

Yet even in this environment, Cage heard two sounds, one high, one low, which he thought were his nervous system and the circulation of his blood. Those sounds were likely evidence of Cage's high blood pressure and damaged hearing – but his point stands. There is no such thing as silence: there is no place in the physical universe in which there is true silence as scientifically defined, a place entirely free of energy. Everywhere in the known universe there are vibrations of waves of different frequencies, from electro-magnetism to gravity waves, from shock-waves to sound-waves.

Which means that John Cage's so-called 'silent piece', *4'33"*, is nothing of the kind. From its first performance in 1952, when the pianist David Tudor performed its three movements by shutting the piano lid for each movement, and raising it in between them, *4'33"* is about turning our listening towards the environmental sounds around us. In that non-silence, there's a world to be discovered.

This is why 'silence' is never truly silent in music. And it's why this pseudo-silence is so present, so energetic, and so vital a force for composers and musicians. They know their pieces and their performances are all temporary projections on a canvas of background quiet – a quietness that is the opposite of an absence, but full of the expectation created by our listening. Silence is the composer's most expressive musical tool, from Joseph Haydn to John Cage.

◀ Joseph Haydn: String Quartet in E flat major, op. 33 no. 2, 'The Joke', finale
◀ Ludwig van Beethoven: Symphony no. 5 in C minor, op. 67
◀ Stella: 'Le Silence'
◀ Michael Pisaro: *Ricefall*
◀ John Cage: *4'33"*

16

What's all that noise?

What's all that noise? Noise is everything you hear in the concert hall that's not the piece of music you're listening to. It's that guy coughing a couple of rows behind you throughout that Bruckner slow movement, the person who claps too soon at the end of a performance of Mahler's Third Symphony. And noise is also all those sounds that you'd really rather weren't there in your daily life: the couple arguing about the popcorn in the cinema; the blare of jet engines as planes descend into the airport on the flight path above you, the low-level hum of the traffic on the main road.

Our cities today are noisy enough to make me give up my piano practice. How can anyone concentrate with all this noise? And my practising isn't noise, by the way: if I choose to make these sounds, however terrible my playing of a Bach fugue, that's not noise, but an intentional consequence of my actions, and therefore, not noisy. But if you try playing the piano next door when I'm trying to sleep – that's another story. Hang on a minute: maybe I'm just as noisy as anyone else . . . And that's the point about noise: it's not just a musical question but a social and even a political issue. One person's noise is another person's manna from sonic heaven. The noises of our cities are necessary products of all of the people who live in them, and everything that's consumed, delivered, and digested there.

And it turns out that without noise, not only would we not have people, cities, or all of the stuff and services we take for granted, we also wouldn't have any music. Because all music is fundamentally noisy. The secret of why acoustic instruments affect us so much is the halo of noise that shimmers above and below and around the note we're hearing. Take a violin: there's the friction of the bow on the string; the resonance of the wood; the way the string interacts with the fingerboard; even the breath of the violinist themselves; the microsounds of the player's finger on the string; an infinitesimal change of pitch or volume or intensity; the grit of sound when the heel of the bow makes contact with the string. These are all 'noises', strictly speaking, since they're not essential to the transmission of the musical fundamentals of pure pitch and accurate rhythm. But they *are* essential to the communication – musical and human – between player and audience. We live in a world of noise – and we should love it. And it's what we do with it – musically and socially, in understanding how our own noise interacts with everyone else's – that counts.

◀ Masonna: *Spectrum Ripper*
◀ Helmut Lachenmann: *Tableau*
◀ Edgard Varèse: *Amériques*
◀ Bob Crosby and the Bobcats: 'Big Noise from Winnetka'
◀ Johann Sebastian Bach: Chaconne, from Partita no. 2 in D minor for solo violin, BWV 1004

17

Turn up the volume, dial up the drama

'It's Oh So Quiet', a song made famous by Björk Guðmunds-dóttir – 'Und jetzt ist es still', in the original 1948 German version – has a lot to tell us about the power of loudness in music. Or rather, the power of relative loudness, relative dynamics, in our music. At the start of the song, it's quiet: it's unchanging, a life untroubled by the tempests of passion and love and intensity of feeling. Until the words 'you fall in love'.

And what happens? Life, music, feelings aren't quiet any more – they're irresistibly loud, with trumpets, a big band, and an infectious groove: instead of pianissimo peacefulness, there are fortissimo passions. 'The sky up above / zing boom / Is caving in' – loudly.

Loudness and quietness in our music aren't only questions of greater and lesser amplitudes of sound-waves – the lower the amplitude, the quieter the sound; the higher, the louder – they're also about meaning and feeling.

In Björk's case, the quiet at the start of the song is anticipation, calm, tranquillity, an intake of breath before the screaming descent and thrill of love's roller coaster. Which is a compositional microcosm of the musical axiom that if you increase or decrease loudness, you're playing and composing not only with musical physics, but with what we all feel as listeners.

49

That's why composers go to extremes to tell musicians how quietly and how loudly to play. Tchaikovsky asks for four degrees of piano – *pppp*, or pianississississimo – at the end of his 'Pathétique' Symphony, demanding his players perform twice as quietly as they conventionally do in other composers' music, reaching a sepulchral abyss of quietness as well as feeling. The American composer Charles Ives requests fifteen levels of forte (fortississississississississississississimo!) at the climax of his *Varied Air and Variations* for solo piano, a piece that parodies a recitalist who offends his audience – not least, by playing too loudly.

And at the very end of Elgar's Second Symphony, there's a chord that grows from a quiet irradiation of sound to a fortissimo, and then fades to quietness again. This gigantic orchestral piece ends in the sounds of its own echo. It's like that feeling at the end of pop tracks, when you follow the chorus into the infinite as they fade to nothing. Elgar had done it decades before. From Björk to Elgar, loudness and softness in our music are all relative – but they're all feeling, too.

◀ Björk: 'It's Oh So Quiet'
◀ Lady Gaga, Andrew Wyatt, Anthony Rossomando, and Mark Ronson: 'Shallow', from *A Star is Born*
◀ György Ligeti: Cello Concerto
◀ Pyotr Ilyich Tchaikovsky: Symphony no. 6 in B minor, 'Pathétique', final movement
◀ Charles Ives: *Varied Air and Variations*

18

The key to keys

Why does music need keys? And how and why are they different from one another? When we're talking about classical music, we hear descriptions all the time of what key pieces are in: Beethoven's Ninth Symphony in D minor; Chopin's D flat major Prelude, the 'Raindrop'; Brahms's Third Symphony in F major. And although this is hardly ever mentioned, keys are essential to music in non-classical genres, too: it's just that we don't usually say, 'Here's The Beatles' "Hey Jude" in F major.' So why do we need our music to be in E major or F sharp major, B or G sharp minor?

The theorist Christian Schubart wrote in his 1806 'Ideen zu einer Ästhetik der Tonkunst' ('Ideas Towards an Aesthetic of Music') that we need different keys to express different emotional and psychological states. Take C major, which uses only the white notes on the piano keyboard. Schubart says in his guide to the keys, 'Its character is: innocence, simplicity, naïvety, children's talk.' (Mozart's 'Jupiter' Symphony does all of that – and much, much more.) Whereas C minor – C major's darker, more troubled cousin, was all about 'Declaration of love and at the same time the lament of unhappy love. All languishing, longing, sighing of the love-sick soul lies in this key,' as in Beethoven's 'Pathétique' piano sonata. If you want some unbridled triumphal glory, you need D major, but for deep depression, F minor. And for the most profound anguish: D sharp minor. 'Feelings of the anxiety of the soul's deepest distress, of brooding despair, of blackest depression, of the most gloomy condition of the soul. Every fear, every hesitation of the shuddering heart, breathes out of horrible D sharp minor. If ghosts could speak, their speech would approximate this key.'

D sharp minor also happens to be the key of Stevie Wonder's joyously grooving 'Superstition' – a track whose character doesn't accord with Schubart's thesis. But then Stevie Wonder is making music in a different era from Schubart and his theories, in a time by which keys had arguably lost their distinctiveness and differences from one another, thanks to the onward march of technology and the subtle arts of equalising musical temperament.

We now live in an era dominated by 'equal temperament' – the way nearly all pianos are tuned today, so we can play music in any key we like, without encountering baleful disharmonies. But in earlier centuries, in earlier tuning systems, music existed in a more diverse and magical world of wolf notes and alchemical commas, which meant there were vivid and sometimes grotesque differences between playing in one key and another.

What's in a key? If you listen to the sweet and sour delights of their differences, of their tuning-based accommodation with the beautiful and creative wound of the Pythagorean comma – that fact of acoustical life that means that any temperament, however supposedly 'equal', can never be fully in tune – you encounter the alchemy of physics and feeling on the resonant secrets of the musical universe.

- Stevie Wonder: 'Superstition', from *Talking Book*
- Wolfgang Amadé Mozart: Symphony no. 41 in C major, K551, 'Jupiter'
- William Byrd: *La Volta*, for keyboard
- Take That: 'Back for Good', from *Nobody Else*
- Johann Sebastian Bach: Partita no. 3 in E major for solo violin, BWV 1006

19

Texture

Do you remember those mystery boxes in natural history museums and Halloween markets that you had to plunge your hand into: was that oozing awfulness a ball of slime or a live slug? Was that a desiccated mound of dead leaves or a live ants' nest? The excitement of pleasure or disgust, sensations transmitted entirely through our tactile experience of texture, and our instant physical and emotional reaction to what we discovered.

And like all those mystery objects, music, too, has texture. It has density and transparency, it has roughness and smoothness, softness and hardness. And just as we have an immediate physical and even emotional reaction to the surfaces of those objects, that's true of musical textures as well: from Henry Purcell's frost-hard sharpness to Maurice Ravel's gossamer filigree, from Frank Sinatra's buttery-smooth vocals to Iannis Xenakis's geological cragginess. Those textures are associated with everything from consolation to anxiety, comfort to danger.

Texture defines the parameters of how layers are built up in a composition – in a track, symphony or string quartet – and how instruments are combined with one another, from the transparency and intimacy of a chamber ensemble to the walls of sound you can create with a full orchestra.

And if we look into the stuff of sound, we find a world that's as physical as the granite slabs of a mountainside or a faux-fur snood against your skin on a wintry day: sound-waves are pressure-waves that are picked up by all of our feeling bodies. Music is viscerally tactile. The perception of sound – not only through hearing, but through all the exquisitely sensitive frequency-receiving membranes of our bodies, from our skin to our nerve-endings – is about 'touching at a distance', as the Canadian composer R. Murray Schafer beautifully put it.

And it's the feeling of that dynamic texturing that gives human-created music its life. The surfaces of sound, their textures, are the opposite of superficial: they're what touches us – the touch of sound, the sound of being touched, being moved.

◀ Iannis Xenakis: *Pithoprakta*
◀ William Barton: *Didgeridoo Solo no. 1*
◀ Maurice Ravel: *Pavane pour une infante défunte*
◀ Frank Sinatra: 'Deep in a Dream'
◀ Henry Purcell: 'Frost Scene', from *King Arthur*

Why is music addicted to bass?

Why are we all addicted to the bass? Our music is built on its bass-lines, whether it's funk or folk, rock 'n' roll or baroque; classical refinement or late-Romantic excess, organ pedal points or minimalist harmonic hypnosis. As musicians and theoreticians have put it over the centuries, the bass is 'the groundwork upon which all musical composition is to be erected'. That was Christopher Simpson in 1667; or as Paul McCartney said: 'None of us wanted to be the bass player. In our minds he was the fat guy who always played at the back.' But without the back, Paul, there can be no front. Gioseffo Zarlino summed it up in 1561: 'The bass part is the foundation of harmony.' Music can have no stable underpinnings without its bass-lines.

They're so important, in fact, that one way of understanding the history of Western music is as a story of what happens to its bass-lines: how they're fixed and freed up, how they root our sense of harmony, rhythm, and comprehensibility – and how, when composers and producers get more adventurous, they start to slip and slide and turn what we thought was a solid musical foundation into a sea of quicksand and instability.

The percussionist Evelyn Glennie has spoken about the visceral necessity of the bass like this: 'Hearing is basically a specialised form of touch. Sound is simply vibrating air which the ear picks up and converts to electrical signals, which are then interpreted by the brain. The sense of hearing is not the only sense that can do this, touch can do this too.' Evelyn knows this well, as a profoundly deaf musician. 'With very low frequency vibration the ear starts becoming inefficient and the rest of the body's sense of touch starts to take over. For some reason we tend to make a distinction between hearing a sound and feeling a vibration. In reality they are the same thing. In the Italian language this distinction does not exist. The verb *sentire* means to hear and the same verb in the reflexive form, *sentirsi*, means to feel.'

There's nothing we feel more strongly than the bass, nothing that roots us in the ecstatic moment of our listening and our dancing more strongly than the siren song of the bass-line, whether it's baroque suites or Toots and the Maytals, Anton Bruckner or Ben E. King.

◀ Johann Sebastian Bach: Prelude, from Suite no. 1 in G major for solo cello, BWV 1007
◀ Toots and the Maytals: '54-46 That's My Number'
◀ Ben E. King: 'Stand By Me'
◀ Miles Davis: 'So What', from *Kind of Blue*
◀ Anton Bruckner: Symphony no. 8 in C minor, first movement

21

The power of one

The power of one line, one song, one melody: music that has no harmony and no accompaniment. The unison: music that's about a single, solo tune, but which is made by communities of singers, not soloists. Because when you have groups of singers all performing the same melody, whether it's Gaelic psalmists in the Western Isles or national anthems at football and rugby matches, whether it's the origins of Western music in the earliest Christian chant or string sections of orchestras, you turn one voice and one tune into a community of voices. It's the paradoxically diverse musical power of the unison.

And there are some acoustic facts of musical and human life that explain the phenomenon. The sonic richness of plainchant in the monastery and football chant in the stadium comes from the fact that no two people can ever sing exactly the same thing. No two renditions of the same notes, the same rhythms, the same words, are precisely alike. There are micro-inflections of rhythm and pitch in the vibrato of the human voice and in the timing of consonants and vowels, whether we're talking about monks, professional singers or football fans. These kaleidoscopic variations are what makes massed communities of singers and instrumentalists performing in unison so richly effective. It's not that we're singing the same thing – it's the differences between us that makes unison singing so powerful.

Singing in unity – yet singing our diversity and differences too. That's where the spirituality of unison singing is found. In the Gaelic psalm traditions of the Free Church in Back, on the north-eastern coast of Lewis, the largest of the Outer Hebrides, there's a special congregational singing that's made from a version of the solo call and unison community response. A precentor leads the congregation, and while they are all singing the same tune, unadorned by harmony, this community in Lewis creates a fantastically rich micropolyphony in which every voice has its own line. If you were to write down what they're doing, you would end up with a score in which every singer would need a different part, even though they're singing the same melody. To transcribe the inflections of pitch, timing and colour as a page of musical notation would need the forensic genius of a virtuosic composer, yet the congregation of Back realises this shimmering musical and spiritual complexity in all their services.

The power of one line: in fact, the alchemy of the unison is the power of the many. It's the simplest but one of the richest experiences we can all we have of melting into a community of singers that's bigger than ourselves. And all we have to do is sing, or play, or perform with others: sharing the same tune, creating an identity and a sound that's more powerful than any of us can be on our own. As Liverpool fans haven't quite sung for decades at Anfield: you'll never sing alone.

◀ Congregation of Back Free Church, Isle of Lewis: Psalm 16
◀ George Enescu: 'Prélude *à l'unisson*', from Suite no. 1 for orchestra
◀ Liverpool Football Club fans at Anfield: 'You'll Never Walk Alone' (Rodgers and Hammerstein)
◀ The crowd at Murrayfield: 'Flower of Scotland' (Roy Williamson)
◀ Louis Andriessen: *Workers Union*

22

The semitone

The humble semitone is the interval that Julie Andrews sings in 'Do-Re-Mi': it's the difference between *mi* and *fa*, and between *te* and *do*. After drinking the former with jam and bread, she's taken back to where she started.

But don't be deceived by Julie's optimism. The semitone is an atomic musical phenomenon. It can become nuclear musical material: because when semitones are used in melodies or to create crunching harmonies when you pile them on top of one another, this smallest and simplest of musical steps can produce the biggest emotional and expressive results.

You can see semitones in the gap between the black notes and their neighbouring white notes on any piano keyboard, middle C to C sharp, B flat to B. Yet this littlest of intervals is the dissonant canker in every scale, the piquant spice of musical imperfection that drives the change from one key to another, from the major mode to the minor.

Composers alchemise that power in so many different ways: in 'Dido's Lament', from Henry Purcell's *Dido and Aeneas*, the music is made from semitones that fall, and fall hard. Dido's song of desolation is created over a bass-line that's a sighing chain of semitones, the land slipping beneath her feet, her tears sighing, falling. The most famous semitones in cinematic history, the double basses' maw of terror in John Williams's score for *Jaws*, down there in the lowest reaches of the orchestra and the unknowable depths of the ocean, trigger a primeval fear. The shark, the semitone, the horror! Jean Sibelius manages a sublime and searing mixture of anguish and resolution at the end of his Seventh Symphony. The final moments of the symphony fulfil Julie Andrews's prediction, bringing us back to 'Do', but the way Sibelius extends the 'Te' in his final cadence turns the meaning of this semitone inside out. 'The most painful scream in C major in all music,' the conductor Simon Rattle called it – and he's got a point.

That gravitational push and pull of resolution is where the semitone derives its expressive power, and composers can use it to keep our feelings on the end of their string, playing with our expectations, giving us everything from morbid consolation to mortal fear, from sensual fulfilment to gut-wrenching dread. They're all using the mighty power of the tiny semitone.

◀ Henry Purcell: 'Dido's Lament', from *Dido and Aeneas*
◀ John Williams: soundtrack for *Jaws*
◀ Franz Schubert: String Quintet in C major, D956, finale
◀ Jean Sibelius: Symphony no. 7
◀ Gustav Mahler: Symphony no. 9, finale

23

The fifth

The perfect fifth: the musical interval between Julie Andrews's *do* and *so* – you'll have heard it countless times. Every orchestral concert starts with a cacophony of fifths, as the string instruments tune. Those strings are tuned in fifths, except for the double basses, and the players fine-tune the distance between them on their strings, focusing in on this physically fundamental and mystically powerful musical space.

The fifth is the most resonant interval after the octave, and it's the carrier and catalyst of so much musical meaning, from fanfares to drones, from punk solos to the virtuosity of Indian classical music, from bagpipe grounds to Anton Bruckner's symphonies.

The essential quality of the fifth allows it to inspire divine contemplations, from the harmonies of early medieval religious chant to the fifth that starts the cosmic journey of Ludwig van Beethoven's Ninth Symphony. But the fifth is also a primal, open sound that makes us want to dance, whether that's the drones under the bagpipes and the reels of Scottish traditions, or the manic whirling of the finale of Joseph Haydn's Symphony no. 104.

Yet the fifth is also the haunted sound of lament over the battlefield. The military bugle is one of the simplest of brass instruments, and in the Last Post, an opening rising fifth calls the living to remember the dead. Another rising fifth is the engine of that evocation of orchestral and galactic space, the sunrise at the start of Richard Strauss's tone-poem *Also sprach Zarathustra*. Funereal fifths, fanfaring fifths, and cosmically epic fifths – composers of all musical traditions have used them in their tunes.

But fifths have another essential role to play in our music, in the way Western harmony works. It all comes from that fact of musical life, that if you keep adding fifths to one another, you end up back where you started. So from C you go to G, then to D, A and E – on and on, cycling through all twelve semitones of the chromatic scale, before getting back to C again. This 'circle of fifths' is a road map that composers can use to get them from one key to the next as smoothly as possible. From Johann Sebastian Bach in his *Well-Tempered Clavier*, to Wolfgang Amadé Mozart's piano concertos, to Lionel Richie's 'Hello', the circle of fifths is everywhere.

And the story of fifths in our music goes on being reinterpreted by today's composers, from Thomas Adès, who makes new harmonic orbits based on fifths in music such as his Violin Concerto, 'Concentric Paths', or John Adams, who sends up the perfect cadence – the most familiar harmonic closure in music, from a chord on the fifth note of the scale back to the home key – in the final part of his deliriously dazzling *Grand Pianola Music*. The story of the fifth is one of inexhaustible musical and human resonance.

◄ The Last Post
◄ Richard Strauss: *Also sprach Zarathustra*, opening
◄ Lionel Richie: 'Hello', from *Can't Slow Down*
◄ Aaron Copland: *Fanfare for the Common Man*
◄ Gundecha Brothers: Raga Behag (Alap)

24

The power of three

Such a simple thing: playing two notes together on a key-board, or singing them in vocal harmonies, to make an interval of a third, a concord between C and E, or the narrower third between D and F. And yet the differences between those intervals of musical space can give us everything from luxurious pleasure to ecstatic melancholy, in the meanings Western musical culture has created for these thirds, major and minor.

We've often interpreted thirds as harmonies that give us sheer, spine-tingling pleasure. That's how they sound in major-key vocal harmonies, like those produced by the singers in Léo Delibes' 'Flower Duet' from *Lakmé*, or the duettists in J. S. Bach's 'Christe eleison' from his Mass in B minor. The sonic gorgeousness of that music is based on the same third-saturated textures that the Everly Brothers used to give their vocals their instantly seductive charm. Graham Nash called the Everly Brothers' thirds 'ghost harmonics', a brilliant description of how completely entwined two voices seem to be when they are singing and harmonising in thirds. That's the conjoining illusion of voices melting and melding into one another that these thirds seems to give us – along with some good old-fashioned goosebumps of sheer pleasure.

But there is another kind of third apart from this major variety, and that's the so-called minor third. It's an interval that's just a semitone smaller than its major cousin, but in that difference lies an ocean of emotional and cultural association. The fundamental chord of C major is made of a major third with a minor third on top: C–E–G. But if you swap those intervals around, and start with a minor third – C–E flat – and put a major on top of that – E flat–G – you create the chord of C minor. And while this is an over-simplification of at least three hundred years of musical history, it's nonetheless true to say that in general, the major triad is associated with more positive emotional states, while minor triads and minor keys tend to evoke sadness or melancholy.

The question is whether this emotional sunshine or rain is something in the nature of the intervals themselves, or whether those feelings are something that we have created for these intervals over the centuries: is it nature or nurture that explains the difference between major and minor? The musical thinker Adam Ockelford has explained that this apparent enculturation may have a biological basis in the micro-acoustics of the resonant spaces of our ear cavities, but whether biological or psycho-musical, it's a fact of musical life that primal spheres of expression can be conjured with the apparent simplicity of combining these thirds together in different ways.

To say nothing of what happens when you combine notes that are precisely three tones apart – F to B natural, or C to F sharp – an interval that the eighteenth century called *diabolus in musica*, the 'devil in music', or as we know it today, the tritone. Pleasure, pain and the devil, all created by combining a handful of notes: the alchemical power of the musical fundamentals of thirds and threes.

- ◀ The Everly Brothers: 'Bye Bye Love' (Felice and Boudleaux Bryant)
- ◀ John Dunstable: *Quam pulchra es*
- ◀ Johannes Brahms: Symphony no. 4 in E minor, op. 98, first movement
- ◀ Cole Porter: 'Ev'ry Time We Say Goodbye'
- ◀ Igor Stravinsky: Suite from *The Firebird*

25

Speed

What makes music sound fast? There are some basic principles that composers and musical cultures have always used, from the Renaissance to the present day. The most obvious musical feature that gives us the feeling of fast motion is rhythms that repeat, obsessively, speedily. The music moves, and it makes us want to move with it, because our bodies resonate in sympathy, so that we want to get our groove onto the dance floor, whether the dance is real, or whether a piece of music sublimates that idea of corporeal motion to go into other dimensions of speeding time and space.

That's what J. S. Bach does in the final movement of his Sixth Brandenburg Concerto, which has a speedy rhythmic regularity as obsessive as any dance track: the string players don't stop their quick-time quavers throughout the whole piece.

But Bach is doing something else. Because the speeds in the Sixth Brandenburg Concerto are, in fact, multiple: there are differently articulated speeds of rhythm, harmonic change and melodic impetus, which spiral against each other. The music moves not only at the speed of the quavers on the surface, but also according to the different rates of change of each of the layers.

And that's a good way of thinking about what speed in music really is: it's relative and multiple. Our perception of speed in music isn't something absolute: it's a fluid sense of momentum, not a precise equation. That's why some supposedly 'slow' music can actually be moving more quickly than perceptually 'fast' pieces. That's one of the illusions of minimalist music, like Steve Reich's *Six Pianos*, whose non-stop quavers pound into your brain. And yet *Six Pianos* is, in reality, a slow piece, because underneath that surface, nothing's changing: the harmony doesn't move, and neither does the collection of pitches the piece uses. *Six Pianos* is radically static music.

On the other hand, superficially 'slow' music, like the 'Adagio espressivo' ('slow, expressively') from Robert Schumann's Second Symphony, with its aching, long-breathed lyricism and slow tempo, has harmonies that change with every beat. So although the surface seems slow-paced, everything in Schumann's music is in motion: its webs of harmony, melody, and motive are in a constant state of dynamic flux.

Beethoven was another composer who knew how to manipulate multiple speeds simultaneously. Towards the end of his life, he discussed his plans for his Tenth Symphony. In this piece, Beethoven said (his words were meticulously recorded by Gerhard von Breuning), he wanted to 'create . . . a new gravitational force'. That might be the most redolent and tantalising sentence in musical history: not only warping speed, but the fabric of space-time in the Tenth Symphony he didn't live to complete. Beethoven, speed-warping compositional relativist.

- ◀ Megadeth: 'Wake Up Dead' (Dave Mustaine)
- ◀ Steve Reich: *Six Pianos*
- ◀ Josh Wink: 'Higher State of Consciousness'
- ◀ Robert Schumann: Symphony no. 2 in C major, op. 61, second movement
- ◀ Pulp: 'Common People', from *Different Class*

26

The simple truth

There is music that's all about clarity and directness of utterance; pieces that are made of a single gesture or a mere handful of notes; music that's content with a solo tune or a single idea, instead of a cosmic flurry of complexity. It's a hard-won simplicity that gives us a magical richness of experience as listeners.

That's what the British composer Howard Skempton does. He has made his musical life about achieving what he calls a 'concrete infinity' in his music: tiny shards for solo piano or accordion, as well as longer pieces for ensemble and orchestra. Instead of composing fistfuls of notes or teeming forests of orchestral scores, he wrote music that seemed almost wilfully simple at a time, in the 1960s and 70s, when composers really weren't supposed to be doing that kind of thing. Music like his *Piano Piece 1969*, which is just a handful of chords, and is only a minute and a half long, reveals this radical simplicity. It's music that's crystalline, multi-faceted, yet immediate in its impact. This rich simplicity comes from the fact that the music gives us time to appreciate each chord in real time, one after the other, at a stately speed. We're asked to hear inside the chords as they happen: our listening is made part of this music, if we're really paying attention to it. Your imagination entwines with the music when you hear the way the top note in the sequence of chords changes, or listen in to the slow melodies created by the inner voices of the harmonies.

It's apparently simple, but this tiny piece resounds with many different interpretations. Like a crystal, *Piano Piece 1969* – or any of the dozens of piano pieces Skempton has composed – is permanent, tangible, a physical presence in the sounding world. Yet it can also be atomised into a kaleidoscope of different ways of hearing it. That's Skempton's 'concrete infinity' in action.

But it's not only Howard Skempton: other composers have achieved this hard-won simplicity at different times: like Mozart, in some of the last music he wrote, the distilled but elusive simplicity of his opera *The Magic Flute*; or Anton Webern, whose musical crystal-kernels are some of the simplest and most organically generative sonic seeds any composer ever crafted, in pieces like his Symphony, op. 21, and Concerto for Nine Instruments, op. 24.

Like the years it takes for great whisky to mature, these things take time. If you're going to get to that place of rich simplicity, where the simple, the unpretentious, the pared-down can resonate as a fragment of infinity – as Howard Skempton can make it do – you need, as the Shaker song says, the gift to be simple. Simplicity is one of the hardest prizes for composers to achieve.

◀ Howard Skempton: *Well, Well Cornelius*; *Chorale* for piano; *Piano Piece 1969*
◀ Laurence Crane: *10,000 Green Bottles*
◀ Anton Webern: Symphony, op. 21
◀ Philip Glass: Violin Concerto no. 1, first movement
◀ The Carpenters: 'Sing' (Joe Raposo)

27

Complexity

Complex music must be difficult music, and difficult music must be unpopular music, and unpopular music must be less fun to listen to. Simple.

Yet complexity is in the ear of the beholder, not in the minds of composers. There are simple ways of hearing the most complex music ever composed, and there are complex ways of hearing the most simple sounds we can imagine.

Take a rainstorm. It's one of the most saturated sounds in the world, so full of microscopic detail in the ultra-complex, quantum-scale percussive polyphony that the falling raindrops make on the surface of water, on the rooftop of a car or a caravan, that we can't process the individual detail and instead are immersed in a tumult of white noise, a frequency-filling noise of bewildering intensity but we turn this microscopically complex sound into a single, simple experience. Or listen to Chris Watson's 'Vatnajökull', the sounds of a glacier in Iceland: nothing simpler to understand, but nothing more unpredictable and complex in terms of what's actually happening, sonically and geologically. Watson's recording reveals a natural soundscape of sublime and terrifying power, yet our ears turn it into a single experience.

And that's what our ears and brains do with music, too.

We might like the rollicking tunes of the finale of Mozart's 'Jupiter' Symphony now, but in the year after Mozart's death, this piece was heard as too complex, too full of details that our brains couldn't possibly process.

And they can't: when Mozart brings all five tunes together at the end of that piece, it's too fast and too dense for us to understand everything that's happening in real time. Instead, we're left surfing the surface of the music, taking in the macro-scale of the symphony while the musicians take care of the details.

John Dunstable's music from the fifteenth century does something similar: we might hear it as a surpassingly gorgeous few minutes of vocal euphony, but Dunstable's motet *Preco preheminenciae* is a virtuoso tour de force of rhythmic ratios and relationships. The vocal lines swirl around each other in orbits of time that are as deeply, deliriously complex as the movement of the planets in the solar system.

At the other end of the spectrum, if you hear the simplest possible piece – a folk melody sung by a solo singer, like Peggy Seeger – and listen in to the infinitely subtle variations of rhythm and tuning, the inflections of her voice, the sounds of her breath and her articulation of the words, you can find a world of dizzying complexity in what seems to be the simplest musical performance. The true richness, the true complexity, is in how we choose to listen, not the sounds themselves.

◀ Chris Watson: 'Vatnajökull', from *Weather Report*
◀ Arnold Schoenberg: Variations for Orchestra, op. 31
◀ John Dunstable: *Preco preheminenciae*
◀ Brian Ferneyhough: *La Terre est un Homme*
◀ Janelle Monáe: 'Don't Judge Me'

28

Tricky timing

Music is made of time. In fact, it's made of lots of times, happening all at once – simultaneously. But there is one number that defines most musical time – four. The great and mighty quadrilateral that seems to hold all before it in the way that most music on the planet is made: if you open up a music sequencer on your computer, it's already counting the music out for you in fours: four beats to the bar, four bars to the phrase, four groups of four bars for the verse: music – quadrilateralised.

Why? Why are we so obsessed with four, and its diminutive cousin, two? Four limbs? Two legs? Marching, walking, left-right, left-right, the symmetry of two times two, our bodies moving in regimented sympathy with the music we're hearing. Yet the squared-off symmetry of our limbs aren't the only numbers we have to count on our bodies; there are other temporal denominators in the rhythms of our lives. We have ten fingers and toes, our calendars are mapped by the seven-day cycle of the week, there are 365 days in most years, and 1,461 in the four-year cycle that includes the leap. We live in a world in which time is marked by irregularly meshing patterns, chaotic cogs of time and numbers churning away against each other.

And music goes to these other non-symmetrical and irregular places too, singing and dancing in fives and sevens: in

Gustav Holst's 'Mars' from *The Planets* and the second movement of Tchaikovsky's 'Pathétique' Symphony, the slow movement of Chopin's First Piano Sonata and the theme tune to *Mission: Impossible*, all in five; in Frank Zappa's 'Don't Eat The Yellow Snow' and 'Oh, Happy We' from Leonard Bernstein's *Candide*, tunes that trip along in a seamless seven-time. And it moves in mash-ups and cut-ups of twos and threes and fractions of beats, overlaid on top of one another, as Igor Stravinsky engineers so in his ballet *The Rite of Spring*.

How does time pass in music? It can be as regular as our machines, or as asymmetrical as the irregular events that shock and upset the metrical grid of our lives. Our lives are lived in a place where time dances and flows in spurts and jolts and then relaxes in oases of long breaths and longer sleep: we move more like Stravinsky's dancers than we do in a straight-ahead quadrilateral march in drill-like conformity.

Music, and musicians, just like the rest of us, are always trying to escape grids and confines: they syncopate the regular pulse, they stretch and warp time, with irregular beats and unconventional patterns that reflect the chaotic, joyous, and relativistic flow of time. Join them in the temporal chaos of their tricky timing.

- ◀ Lalo Schifrin: theme from *Mission: Impossible*
- ◀ Gustav Holst: 'Mars', from *The Planets*
- ◀ Meshuggah: 'New Millennium Cyanide Christ', from *Chaosphere*
- ◀ György Ligeti: *Poème symphonique*, for 100 metronomes
- ◀ Christopher Tye: *In nomine* XIII – 'Trust'

29

Swing, rubato and bounce

Swing: that musical quality that starts a chemical chain reaction in your brain that makes your feet tap and your whole body move. As Fats Waller supposedly answered to the question, 'What is swing?': 'If you got to ask, you ain't got it.'

So can we define swing as well as feel it? It's not as easy as it is to experience it in music from Duke Ellington to Jean-Baptiste Lully, from Billie Holiday to Frédéric Chopin – yes, classical music swings too, even if the phenomenon has been called different things like *notes inégales* and *tempo rubato* over the centuries. The *New World Encyclopedia* attempted a definition: swing is 'any time a note is not accentuated in a "straight" way, exactly on the beat, but rather slightly before or slightly after, a special kind of push or accentuation is given to the beat, making it feel "bouncy".'

And Gunther Schuller, who wrote an entire book on *The Swing Era*, said that if you want 'to learn what swing is and how it sounds, the [Oscar] Peterson Trio's recording of "How High the Moon" provides the ultimate lesson. It is not possible to listen to this performance without wanting to move one's feet, hand, body in time to the beat.' But Schuller also proved how all this was happening using spectrograph imaging: he came up with forensically detailed graphs of the way the musicians played, with so much information about the texture, timbre, timing, volume and pitch of each note, that if you were to represent it accurately, a single second of music would need sixteen feet of paper to show it all.

Schuller looked at just seven notes played by Ray Brown, the bassist in the Oscar Peterson trio, and proved that Brown is making a virtuosically subtle dance with the beat and with the length of the notes he's plucking on the bass, using a huge variety of touch and timing to change the duration of everything he plays. Schuller's spectrographs prised apart the atoms of these notes to reveal the always dynamic, ever-changing quanta of swing.

But classical music has also been swinging for centuries. In so many traditions of classical musical performance, the magic is found not in what the score says, but in what the performers are doing differently to bring it alive – playing not on the beat, but before, after, and in between. In the seventeenth and eighteenth centuries, you weren't always supposed to play rhythms in a regular way, but to animate them with baroque music's equivalent of swing: turning drill-like repeated quavers on the page into swinging, unequal triplets in living, swinging performance, in music from Lully and Couperin to J. S. Bach and Handel. In the nineteenth century, *tempo rubato* – 'robbed time' – meant the same principle extended to whole pieces of music, from Johann Strauss's waltzes to Chopin's Nocturnes, so that the pulse of the music is always changing, phrase to phrase, melody to melody, section to section.

So let's swing again, like classical music always used to, and like jazz always does. Ivie Anderson and Duke Ellington had it right in 1932: 'It don't mean a thing (if it ain't got that swing).'

- ◀ Oscar Peterson Trio: 'How High the Moon'
- ◀ Fletcher Henderson and His Orchestra: 'Big John's Special'
- ◀ Count Basie: 'Easy Does It'
- ◀ Johann Strauss II: *The Blue Danube* (Vienna Philharmonic, Carlos Kleiber, 1989)
- ◀ Ludwig van Beethoven: Symphony no. 4 in B flat major, op. 60, first movement (Berlin Philharmonic, Wilhelm Furtwängler, 1943)

30

Riffs, loops and ostinati

They're so stubborn, so unchanging, so obsessive – but we need them in our music so much: 'ostinati', the plural of 'ostinato', the Italian word meaning 'stubborn'. That suggests something that's obsessively repeated, a pattern in our favourite pieces of music that stays the same while the rest of a song or a concerto's vocals, musical lines or arrangements are free to change around them. Ostinati in classical music, riffs in pop music, or loops in sampling and minimalism: these repetitive foundations keep the musical world turning, from Donna Summer to Dire Straits, from Johannes Brahms to Johann Pachelbel.

But why? Unlike ostinati, or riffs, or bass-lines that don't change throughout a whole piece of music, our bodies, our brains and our perceptions are developing and changing all the time, so why are we so attracted to pieces of music that are built on machine-like repetition? As the American composer Julius Eastman puts it in the title of a twenty-four-minute piece that's built on one musical fragment, we want our music to Stay On It.

It's as if we're human-machine cyborgs, who want to groove to these riffs, ostinati of unchanging, time-stopping obsessiveness, to escape our worlds of change, ageing and decay, for precious musical minutes in which time is stubbornly held in place by the obsessive machinations of the ostinato. Are ostinati machines or flesh-and-blood musical creations?

Donna Summer and Giorgio Moroder prove that the answer is both. In 'I Feel Love', released in 1977, they made music that's right on the knife-edge between human and mechanical pleasure. Donna Summer's vocals inhabit a halo of sensual dreaminess, over the ostinati of Moroder's synthesiser. And that unforgettable synth line is a two-beat pleasurable pounding into your musical synapses that's repeated continuously throughout the track, strobing across your speakers. That's all there is in the material of this song: Donna Summer's voice is suspended into a trance state by this hypnotic ostinato, and we're suspended with her. The magic of this song – which was expanded by the producer Patrick Cowley into a sixteen-minute pleasure zone – is that it makes us feel that out-of-control trippiness of falling in love, by taking that one moment of the ostinato and extending it into the infinite.

Sex and machines: mind you, using only the machinery of the orchestra, Maurice Ravel had been there, done that in 1928 in *Boléro*. This is a piece made of two tunes, one rhythmic ostinato, and nothing else, repeated over and over again in an orchestral crescendo of mechanised eroticism that lasts fifteen minutes. And Igor Stravinsky had done something similar in 1913 in his ballet *The Rite of Spring*: the chosen one, the girl who must dance herself to death, is extinguished in the 'Sacrificial Dance' by a terrifying pile-up of ostinato patterns.

Ostinati, riffs, loops: pleasure-givers we want to repeat and repeat, which also threaten to turn into infernal machines, whether tragic or electronic. Always the same, but always different. Take it from Julius Eastman: Stay On It – Stay On It – Stay On It – Stay On It – Stay On It . . .

◀ Gloria Gaynor: 'Never Can Say Goodbye' (Clifton Davis)
◀ Julius Eastman: *Stay On It*
◀ Maurice Ravel: *Boléro*
◀ Donna Summer: 'I Feel Love' (Summer/Moroder/Bellotte)
◀ Igor Stravinsky: *The Rite of Spring*

31

Transcendence

How does music take us to transcendence? How does it take us out of ourselves, how does it give us a vision of the beyond? One of the signature realisations of a musical paradise is Gabriel Fauré's Requiem. The final movement of the Requiem – 'In Paradisum' – is a celestial musical lullaby, crowned by ethereal organ arpeggios, and its serene vocal lines breathe an atmosphere of radiant calmness. This luminously transcendent music is the subtle climax of the whole work, a symbol of a slowly achieved acceptance of mortality; a cosseting hymn to the eternal peace that Fauré suggests awaits us all.

Yet music can realise other kinds of transcendence that aren't so meditatively melodic: ecstasies of the body, and of intoxicated, mind-altering intensity. Music can transfigure our perception of the world through an excess of rhythmic obsession and whirling energy, an approach that connects the whirling dervishes of Turkish traditions to shamanic rituals in Siberia and South Korea, and which has a terpsichorean echo in the genre of trance in clubs of the 1980s and 90s, in which DJs would metaphorically – and literally – induce narcotic transcendence in thousands of clubbers. That's an energy that Thomas Adès transfigures in his orchestral work from 1997, *Asyla*, whose third movement is punningly called 'Ecstasio', in which dizzying layers of orchestral texture and rhythmic strata grind against each other. Adès's piece turns the orchestra itself into a musically intoxicated collective.

But arguably the most extreme orchestral transcendence of them all comes from 1915. At the end of his life, the Russian composer Alexander Scriabin was planning a piece that would bring about the end of the world. *Mysterium* would be a fusion of music, dancing, and apocalyptic visions, as well as intoxicating perfumes and mists. It was to be performed in the Himalayas over an entire week, and it would be followed by the end of the world-order, and the birth of a new kind of human being, a 'nobler' vision of humanity, according to Scriabin.

It's no surprise – and it's probably just as well for the rest of humanity – that Scriabin didn't finish *Mysterium*, or get anywhere close. Just fifty-three pages of musical sketches were completed by the time of his death, for the prefatory act that would precede the week-long apocalyptic ritual of *Mysterium* itself.

But decades later, the Soviet composer Alexander Nemtin turned those fragments into a three-hour orchestral and choral epic: the *Preparation for the Final Mystery*. And it turns out that the end of the world sounds like excess – and more of it. Nemtin uses a huge orchestra, a wordless choir, intoning harmonies that are completely saturated, indulging every scintilla of colour in the notes an orchestra can play. Nemtin's music can be both radiantly slow and serene, but it's also as obsessively propulsive and energised as trance. It's music that wants to have it all, to express it all – as it needs to, if it's going to bring about the apocalypse.

So whether it's serene, whether it's rhythmic, whether it's narcotic or ecstatic, the goal of so much music is to take us to transcendence. And it does, because there's an essential magic in the way that music works on our brains and bodies. That

magic is inexplicable, ineffable; yet it's tangibly, transcendent-
ally there in any music that takes us to ecstasy – and beyond.

- ◀ Hildegard von Bingen: *O vis aeternitatis*
- ◀ John Tavener: *The Protecting Veil*
- ◀ Binary Finary: '1998'
- ◀ Terry Riley: *Persian Surgery Dervishes*
- ◀ Alexander Scriabin/Alexander Nemtin: *Preparation for the Final Mystery*

32

Searching for paradise

Is there a definitive sound of the sacred? For all the vast diversity of religious musics and rituals all over the world, there is one musical feature that's common to so many religious traditions, from Buddhism to Christianity, Judaism to Islam: it's our voices, singing, declaiming, and chanting melodic shapes, as we commit religious texts to memory through the sounding mechanisms of our bodies.

In the early Christian church, this repertoire of chants was how the liturgy and the scripture was disseminated, so the early church was full of singers. It's possible to hear this music from as far back as the fourth century, in the Ambrosian chant of the Bishop of Milan. The form of these chants is a simple call and response: a single voice intones a melody, which is then taken on in the tune and text of the choir of monks. Their voices would reverberate through the spaces of early church buildings, with their vaulted ceilings and architecture designed to humble the human and glorify the godly.

This kind of singing developed into the repertory we now call Gregorian chant, after Pope Gregory I, who made major efforts in the sixth century to compile chants according to the services of the Roman Catholic liturgical year. They were written down and codified with ever greater precision as music developed as a literary as well as sonic language throughout the later first millennium, and are still sung today,

And across different religions, the practice of chanting is about getting these texts, and these ideas, into our bodies. Singing, in that sense, sacralises us; it literally makes us sacred, since we're the vessels through which the word of God – Yahweh, Allah, the Hindu deities – is voiced.

By the thirteenth century in the Christian church, musical techniques had been refined into an efflorescence of compositional possibility. In Notre Dame in Paris, the composer Pérotin made music in not just one but four simultaneous vocal parts in a piece called *Viderunt omnes* ('All have seen'). It takes the singers around a minute to get to the second syllable of the text, such is the joyful dazzle and sensual complexity of Pérotin's music. It's a piece that doesn't aim to 'set' these words so much as to turn them into experience: we hear the music unfurl in front of us, ever more beautiful, ever more extravagant, especially in the super-resonant cathedral for which it was written. The meaning of the words in *Viderunt omnes* – the final line is 'Rejoice in the Lord' – is turned into a musical rejoicing, a transcendence of liturgical function into aesthetic abandon.

Viderunt omnes is just one of the countless proofs of the ties that bind the musical to the sacred: when our souls are full of faith, we need to sing; and when we are full of music as performers or listeners, we might feel a mysterious presence – ethereal and difficult to define but indelibly, unforgettably experienced, the same phenomenon that any religious person would call divine. This is the miracle of music and the sacred: through their mutual resonance, across time and tradition, we are enchanted.

- *Paravi lucernam Christo meo* (Christian chant)
- *Mi Sheoso Nisim* (performed by cantor Berele Chagy)
- *Pachyu Nghachhya* (Nepalese shamanic music performed by Yarjung Tamu, Man Bhadur, Jaman Sing, Thau Bhadur)
- *Raag Bhatiyar* (Hindustani raag performed by Rakesh Chaurasia, Sunil Das, Bhavani Shankar)
- Pérotin: *Viderunt omnes*

33

The blues

We've all got the blues: from the 'Blue Devils', as the sixteenth century had it – an exquisite and terrible suffering turned into the sharply sweet melancholy of John Dowland's songs and Claudio Monteverdi's madrigals – to the consecration of the blues as a musical genre in the twentieth, in recordings like those made by the King of the Blues, Robert Johnson, in the Mississippi Delta.

The whole history of popular music literally has the blues, since blues was born from a fusion of African, American, and European influences and given voice by generations of enslaved people. This communal and specifically African American music has been given to the world. And taken by the world too: composers from Maurice Ravel to Igor Stravinsky and musicians from Mick Jagger to Elvis Presley have recognised the blues, removed it from its original context, and remade it in their own image. And, almost certainly, in yours: we all love the blues, just as we all need and love to be blue from time to time.

How does music sing the blues – how have blue notes expressed our melancholy over the centuries? There turn out to be some amazing coincidences across time and culture within music's alchemical expression of our possession by the blue

Beelzebubs of melancholia, so that the same combination of notes is used to hymn the blues whether you're Billie Holiday or Claudio Monteverdi.

Across the centuries, across cultures, John Dowland's 'Flow, my tears' and Robert Johnson's 'Kind Hearted Woman Blues' use the same descending sequence of notes as a melodic and harmonic incarnation of the blues: a single singer and a lute in 1596, a guitar in the 1930s, voicing a similar aching melancholy.

Music has always had the blues: and almost whatever music you love the most, you're bound to be addicted to melancholic, tear-strewn musical descents. The final movement of Pyotr Ilyich Tchaikovsky's 'Pathétique' Symphony is the ultimate symphonic *lacrimae*, with its tunes and harmonies that descend and then burrow further downward into new regions of keening melancholy. Tchaikovsky concentrates and apotheosises the power of the descending musical lament, and makes a symphony that sears and burns with its falling tears. Tchaikovsky had the blues – and so did Robert Johnson and Bessie Smith, and so does Robert Cray. We're all falling down tear-strewn musical descents with them – and yet we can never get enough of it. The paradoxical power of the blues in music? It never makes you blue.

◀ B. B. King: 'Three O'Clock Blues'
◀ Robert Johnson: 'Kind Hearted Woman Blues'
◀ John Dowland: 'Flow, my tears'
◀ Pyotr Ilyich Tchaikovsky: Symphony no. 6 in B minor, 'Pathétique', final movement
◀ Bessie Smith: 'A Good Man is Hard to Find'

34

Improvisation

What is musical freedom? If it exists anywhere, it's in the improvisation-led traditions of music-making, from Hindustani cultures to jazz solos, to the entire twentieth- and twenty-first-century genre of 'free improvisation'.

But what does it mean to be free? If we can talk about music that's free, does that mean there's a music that *isn't* free, that's imprisoned, or at least contained – by written-down notation, say, like so much Western classical music?

The pianist and composer Frederic Rzewski asked the saxophonist Steve Lacy to sum up the difference between composition and improvisation in fifteen seconds. Here's what Steve said: 'In fifteen seconds the difference between composition and improvisation is that in composition you have all the time you want to decide what to say in fifteen seconds, while in improvisation you have fifteen seconds.'

It is an elegant definition, but it might be more complicated than that: what if somebody wanted to repeat your fifteen-second improvisation? Would it still be an improvisation then? They would be playing it in the recreative way that classical musicians work – performing from notes on a page, written, usually, by someone else.

Yet there are places where improvisation is still an essential part of classical music practice – the cadenzas, the spaces for solos that form part of concertos by Mozart, Haydn, Beethoven and their contemporaries. If you're an imaginative pianist or violinist today, you'll do what Mozart would have done, and come up with your own cadenzas, a combination of tricks you've worked out and practised in advance, and inspirations that come to you in the moment.

But that kind of improvisation within a style is what Derek Bailey – guitarist, improviser, and chronicler of improvisation – calls 'idiomatic improvisation'. That means it's bounded by the conventions of a style or a historical period. What works for a Mozart cadenza won't work for a Duke Ellington number, or a Louis Armstrong song, or a Sidney Bechet cut.

Which is where the idea of 'free improvisation' – or in Derek Bailey's term, 'non-idiomatic improvisation' – comes in. In this music-making, the only parameter is that there are no parameters at all, only the possibilities of what a group of musicians can do: a musical territory that's just as immeasurable as that suggests.

But there are limits here too: if 'free improvisation' is a tradition that's made by avoiding any references to pre-existing musical idioms, then by definition, it's constrained. It can't sound 'classical', it can't sound like 'jazz', it can't sound like 'pop', so there's a lot this supposedly free improvisation can't do.

Yet even if it's a tautology, 'free improvisation' has produced the most compelling realisations of musical freedom that I know – from the bass-playing of Joëlle Léandre to the kits for improvisation created by the saxophonist and composer John Zorn. As the writer and musician David Toop puts it: dive into the maelstrom of improvisation yourself, and discover new worlds of freedom.

- ◀ Spontaneous Music Ensemble: *Karyōbin*
- ◀ Johann Sebastian Bach: Brandenburg Concerto no. 5, BWV 1050.2, first movement
- ◀ Jimi Hendrix: 'Bold As Love'
- ◀ Derek Bailey: 'When Your Lover Has Gone'
- ◀ Joëlle Léandre and India Cooke: 'Just Now Two'

35

Folk music

Here's a starter for ten: who wrote the first folk song? Folk songs seem to belong to all of us, but it's only logical to imagine that somebody, somewhere, must at some point have sung 'Barbara Allen' or 'Dives and Lazarus', 'Shallow Brown' or 'Brigg Fair' for the very first time, before they became part of our cultural musical memory.

We do know that 'Brigg Fair' was first preserved in sound in 1908, in a performance by the seventy-three-year-old Joseph Taylor. He was recorded by the Australian composer Percy Grainger, part of a movement of folk-song collectors who carted gigantic wax-cylinder recording devices around the English countryside to record these tunes for posterity and to inspire a new confidence and sense of identity within British music.

Joseph Taylor didn't invent this tune, which had been in his life for decades, and whose precise origins are unknown – yet there's no doubt when we hear him singing 'Brigg Fair' that we're hearing a folk song. But what does that actually mean? What is it about this tune that signals 'folk song' to us? Is it because it sounds as though it comes from an earlier time, from some imagined pastoral pre-modernity? Or is it something distinctive about the way its notes move? And who are the 'folk' we're talking about? Is folk music mine? Is it yours?

Cecil Sharp founded the English Folk Dance and Song Society, and he may have collected the first folk song in the twentieth century, as he overheard a gardener called John England – John England! – singing 'The Seeds of Love' in 1903. Here's Sharp's definition of folk music, published in *English Folk Song, Some Conclusions* in 1907: 'The unconscious music of the folk has all the marks of fine art: that it is wholly free from the taint of manufacture, the canker of artificiality . . . it is transparently pure and truthful, simple and direct in its utterance.'

There are a lot of ideological goings-on in that sentence. 'The folk': who are they? Working-class labourers? Probably not the aristocratic upper echelons in any case, and not the urban middle class or intelligentsia. The folk, in Sharp's formulation, are out there in the fields, they're not the 'us' in our drawing rooms and chintzy salons. The folk are there to have collecting done to them, so that their music – however simple and direct, and however much Sharp valued those qualities in singers like John England – could be preserved, gentrified and used as the basis of new compositions.

Wind forward to our own time, and what is the real folk music of so many Western cultures? It's more likely to be Adele or Ed Sheeran than 'Greensleeves', but we don't think of pop music as 'folk music', when in reality, in terms of who's singing it and to whom it belongs, that's exactly what it is.

That gets us to a better definition of folk music, I think: folk music is any music that we feel is ours because we sing it and perform it, which belongs to us as an unconscious reality of our lives. Which makes the question of who first wrote the tunes pretty redundant. Who wrote the first folk song? It just doesn't matter. What matters instead is what we do with it.

- ◀ 'Brigg Fair', performed by Joseph Taylor
- ◀ Frederick Delius: *Brigg Fair*, an English Rhapsody for orchestra
- ◀ Adele: 'Someone Like You'
- ◀ Peter Maxwell Davies: *Farewell to Stromness*
- ◀ Ralph Vaughan Williams: *Fantasia on 'Greensleeves'*

A COLLECTION OF INSTRUMENTS,
INNOVATIONS AND VOICES

36

The French horn unwound

It's partly a brilliant, shiny, brassy instrumental reality, but it's also a talisman of myth and legend, which sounds regions beyond our daily lives: of Elfland, of fairy-tale, of the ancient hunt: I mean, of course, the horn.

The French horn, that is, if you're an English speaker; in every other language, it's just the unadulterated 'horn'. The horn conjures the sound of Romanticism in the nineteenth century, transmitting the nature-worshipping dreams of composers from Schumann to Brahms to Wagner in their chamber music, symphonies and operas. And in the twentieth and twenty-first centuries, the horn's ability to sound out its realm of natural harmonics, and its suggestion of new musical spaces, has inspired composers' wildest musical dreams. In Thea Musgrave's Horn Concerto, four off-stage orchestral horns are controlled by the horn soloist on stage, re-wilding the dynamics of the concerto form. Tansy Davies's *Forest*, pitting four horns against the orchestra, is music that turns the orchestra into a wildwood: the hornists are cast as human beings and hunters in Davies's musicscape, and they are gradually engulfed and overwhelmed by the forest, returning to nature by the end of the piece.

Yet the predecessors of today's artfully wound instruments that sit up there resplendent in the lights of the concert platform, behind the strings and the woodwind, are much more primitive military and hunting horns, which you can still hear in France. These horn-ancestors are celebrated by the group Les Trompes de France. They made a record with the Academy of St Martin in the Fields under the unflappable baton of Neville Marriner, and in a suite by the early-eighteenth-century composer Jean-Joseph Mouret, the Trompes make a joyous incursion of violently uncontrollable sound and fury into the urbane world of the Academy's musicianship. No bull ever rearranged a china shop so effectively: Les Trompes' archaic hunting horns destroy any sense of decorum or musical taste in a celebration of untameable horn-ic wildness.

But this unforgettable outing by the Trompes de France is only an extreme version of what every subsequent composer does with the horn in later orchestral music. Horns always bring the untameable, untunable outdoors into the cosseted confines of the concert hall, conjuring worlds of forests, chase and nature, idylls real and imagined.

Richard Wagner realised his most vivid and imaginative orchestral visions through his writing for the horns of his orchestras. Throughout the four music dramas of the *Ring* cycle, Wagner uses the horn as sound, symbol, and as a dramatic character in its own right. Horns sound the depths of the Rhine at the very start of the cycle; and a solo horn is Siegfried's magical instrument, whose call conjures his connection with the natural world and lures the dragon Fafner to his death.

But it's not just Siegfried – we all respond to the horn's calls in some ancient part of our shared cultural and evolutionary memory. The hunts may have gone, but the horns are still calling us on; cajoling, galloping, yelping, into the musical wildwoods, setting the wild echoes flying in our imaginations –

just as Benjamin Britten releases those sounds in his *Serenade* for tenor, horn, and strings.

◀ Johannes Brahms: Horn Trio in E flat major, op. 40, first movement
◀ Donald Swann: 'Ill Wind' (Michael Flanders and Donald Swann)
◀ Jean-Joseph Mouret: *Suite de Symphonies* no. 2, first and second movements (Les Trompes de France/Academy of St Martin in the Fields/Neville Marriner)
◀ Carl Maria von Weber: Overture to *Oberon*
◀ Richard Wagner: 'Siegfried's Horn Call', from Act 2 of *Siegfried*
◀ Thea Musgrave: Horn Concerto

37

The double bass

The double bass is much more than the musical elephant in the room (even if a solo double bass is the sound that Camille Saint-Saëns chooses to depict the pachyderm plodder in his *Carnival of the Animals*). These superhuman sculptures for music, the biggest and lowest of the string instruments, create a literal and physical wall of sound when there are groups of them playing together in the huge orchestras of a Mahler symphony or a Wagner music drama; the double bass has been a concerto soloist in classical music since the eighteenth century, and the virtuosity of jazz bassists like Willie Dixon and Charles Mingus makes the instrument a plucked and grooved inspiration that keeps music moving.

You can as easily hide a double bass as you can fit a camel through the eye of a needle, so it's a strange quirk that the origins of the bass are a music-historical mystery. Whereas the shapes of the viola and cello make it obvious that they are scaled-up violins, basses, by contrast, have sloping shoulders to allow the player to reach down the strings. They're also built proportionately wider and deeper than every other string instrument, to allow the long sound-waves produced by their low notes space and time to resonate properly.

In fact, the double bass is a physical relic of an older family

of string instruments: the viols, all of which had those charac-
teristic shoulders and deeper sounding cavities. The richness
and resonance of the viol family dominated string music for
two centuries, before the glitter and dazzle of the violin an-
nounced a new musical era in Italy from the 1500s. Which
means that whenever you look at a double bass on a concert
platform or in a jazz club, you're looking much further back
in musical time than you would be with those recent upstarts,
the violin, viola or cello.

But there's no need for special pleading when it comes to the
double bass's place in the story of music over the last five hundred years. If there were no double basses to root orchestral
textures from Bach's cantatas to Haydn's symphonies, it's not
only that our music would sound bass-bereft, it couldn't have
been composed the same way. European music was conceived
from the bass-line up: without those sonorous regions of register and harmony, the music we call classical could never have
existed. And it's not only within orchestral textures, because
the double bass stepped out into the limelight as a soloist, in
hundreds of concertos written by composers like Johann Baptist Vanhal and Carl Ditters von Dittersdorf, and in the surreal
virtuosity of the repertoire written by the nineteenth-century
composer and double bass virtuoso, Giovanni Bottesini.

To find real creative freedom in twentieth-century bass-
playing, it's in jazz where the bass found a new voice, and
pioneered new approaches from Jimmy Blanton's slap bass
– Blanton made the first-ever records of piano and bass duos
with Duke Ellington – to Charles Mingus's alchemical imagination as player and composer.

As well as those virtuosos and pioneers, there's something
primal in our relationship with the bass. The double bass isn't
just the size of a large human being – it *is* a musical body. You

want to be as close as you can to that sound: you feel that your whole body is being plucked and bowed in sonic and emotional sympathy by the sounds that basses make, from gigantic orchestral bass sections in Strauss or Bruckner, to soloists playing Mingus or Ellington. We need to feel those vibrations from those huge resonating bodies: all hail the bass.

- ◀ Johann Baptist Vanhal: Concerto for double bass in D major
- ◀ Giovanni Bottesini: Concerto no. 2 in B minor for double bass
- ◀ Duke Ellington and Jimmy Blanton: 'Mr J. B. Blues'
- ◀ Charles Mingus: 'Haitian Fight Song'
- ◀ Joëlle Léandre: 'To Day and To Morrow'

38

The bagpipes

From where I grew up in Glasgow, you could hear them on a summer wind, even though they were playing about a mile away, making a sound so droningly, skirlingly elemental that even the outside world seemed too small for their massed chanting and dancing. What serried ranks of instruments – miraculous for some, infernal for others – could make this gigantic, heaven-storming racket?

It was, of course, the bagpipes – Great Highland Bagpipes, to be precise – endless phalanxes of them at competitions in Bellahouston Park, in bands from all over Scotland and all over the world, playing their strathspeys and reels in uniquely tartaned outfits, regaling us in their regalia.

Yet in fact, there are hundreds of different kinds of bagpipe that have been played for a thousand years and more in a continuous arc of piping prosperity from Scandinavia to Southern Italy, through the Middle East and into India. The pipes are so ubiquitous, yet so diverse, from the brightly pungent Macedonian gaida to the sweet-voiced Calabrian zampogna, or the bucolic Hungarian duda.

And the pipes have added an essential earthiness and piquancy to classical and pop repertoires, in impressions of the French *musette* in operas by Rameau or the German Dudelsack in

Haydn's symphonies, to Peter Maxwell Davies's pipe-festooned dawn in his *An Orkney Wedding, with Sunrise*. And the Great Highland Pipes and their smaller cousins, the uilleann pipes from Ireland, give an epic scale and intimate soulfulness to songs from Kate Bush to Tears for Fears, AC/DC to Paul McCartney: imagine 'Mull of Kintyre' without the pipes – impossible!

Given all that internationalism and cross-genre creativity, how did the pipes become an icon of Scotland in the eighteenth and nineteenth centuries? There's a clear demarcation in the repertoires of the Great Highland Bagpipes, between the *ceòl beag*, in Gaelic – the 'small music', of dances, waltzes, strathspeys and reels – and the *ceòl mòr*, the 'big music', also known as *pibroch*. This 'big music' is a repertoire of single-movement, multi-section compositions, lasting from five to twenty-five minutes, which have been handed down through generations of pipers in Scotland for over three hundred years. *Pibroch* is the classical music of the pipes, a repertoire of more than two hundred tunes, with more still being composed to-day, which are the bedrock of any piper's study. It's a genre with its own rules of structure and expression, whose composition, transmission and performance constitute the most exposed and the most demanding of all of the pipe's traditions.

And I need the pibroch in my life: these pieces make a sound as vivid and as physical as the landscapes they soar and sear in. The pibroch's keening intensity, in dozens of pieces made to commemorate personal and communal loss, sounds a sharply moving musical lament. But it's never a sound of self-indulgent sorrow. Instead, in pibroch it's as if the glaciated geology of the Highlands itself could sing, from the blazing dazzle of light on water to the glint of snow and ice and granite; the heart of the mountains turned inside out to reveal these epic, austere, but human songs.

◀ Ulrich Roever and Michael Korb: 'Highland Cathedral'
◀ Peter Maxwell Davies: *An Orkney Wedding, with Sunrise*
◀ Kate Bush: 'The Sensual World'
◀ AC/DC: 'It's a Long Way to the Top (If You Wanna Rock 'n' Roll)', from *T.N.T.*
◀ Patrick Mor MacCrimmon: 'Lament for the Children'

39

The orchestra

There's a lot we take for granted in the sound, sociology and story of the symphony orchestra. Why does it look the way it does? Why are there all those strings, woodwinds, brass players, and a handful of percussionists, in the conventional orchestral configuration you can experience all over the world? Does the shape of the orchestra result from composers pushing the boundaries of what they wanted to hear, or from the economic and technological limitations of the time and place?

Let's start, as so often, in Ancient Greece. Because it was there that the term 'orchestra' was coined: and it didn't mean makers of sounds. The 'orchestra', rather, was the circular patch of ground on which the players would perform – so it was a shared, public space. And the modern story of how orchestras have developed, from the seventeenth to the twenty-first centuries, is also a story of how music moves from private to ever more public environments: from aristocratic salons and exclusive theatres to bigger concert halls, into new genres and new media, from disco to hip-hop to video games and virtual reality. Orchestras are owned by their audiences and their consumers as much as they are by their musicians.

More time-travelling: to Mantua in Italy in 1607, and the premiere of a piece of music theatre by Claudio Monteverdi.

L'Orfeo – *Orpheus* – is an operatic myth of the origins of music that also incarnates an idea of the orchestra. Monteverdi calls for a particular group of *stromenti* for the instrumental drama-tisation of *L'Orfeo*. Monteverdi wanted the players' violins, sackbuts, lutes and organs to be associated with different char-acters, moods and situations. The instrumentarium of *L'Orfeo* is one of the birthplaces of the orchestra, because it creates a variety of sounds from sheer dramatic necessity. The origins of the European orchestra make it a machine for colour, emotion and drama.

But Monteverdi's music didn't define a standardised set of instruments. And that remains the case throughout the seven-teenth and most of the eighteenth centuries, because the music of Bach, Haydn and Mozart was written for whatever instruments were most available to them in their churches and courts, and among their freelancing friends.

Yet for all the huge diversity of the shape and sound of the orchestra, by the late eighteenth century, it starts to look more and more like your local symphony orchestra's set-up. The or-chestral soundworld is based on a multitude of string players, because the more strings you have, the louder – and the softer – you can play, and the more show-stopping the effects you can produce – like the famous 'Mannheim rocket', a collec-tive crescendo that dazzled anyone who heard it in the eight-eenth century. The nineteenth and early twentieth centuries continue this story of expansion across every other section of the orchestra, from woodwind to brass, and lastly, to percus-sion, in music from Beethoven to Berlioz, Bruckner to Mahler, Richard Strauss to Stravinsky.

Yet it's really the orchestra's continual flexibility and versatil-ity, the fact that it's always changing, that make it ever-present in all of our musical lives, whether we're hearing the orchestra as underscore, backing track, or as the main event of a concert or opera.

Above all, orchestras are public: they belong to all of us. The history of the orchestra has produced some of the loudest and quietest, the most thrilling and the most moving sounds that humanity has ever made. And by listening to them, we're joining in with them. As listeners, we're made more ourselves by joining in with their collective musical work. We are orchestra!

◀ Benjamin Britten: *The Young Person's Guide to the Orchestra*
◀ Claudio Monteverdi: *L'Orfeo*
◀ Joseph Haydn: Symphony no. 22 in E flat major, 'The Philosopher', first movement
◀ Richard Strauss: 'Des Helden Walstatt' (The Hero in Battle), from *Ein Heldenleben*
◀ Alexander Mosolov: *The Iron Foundry*

40

What's the point of the conductor?

A moot point, a phoney profession, the acme of charlatanism: orchestral conductors have been called all of those, and worse, and not only by the musicians who have to play for them. Why is orchestral culture so in thrall to these baton-wielding men and women, who don't make a sound but who seem to have so much power over the musicians in front of them? Why can't the musicians do it without them?

In fact, they can. And it's not only Persimfans, the world's first unconducted large-scale symphony orchestra in Soviet Russia, that proves the point. Orchestras don't need conduct-ors to play their instruments. But conductors are useful, be-cause they have helped to co-ordinate a large body of people in front of them, since the orchestra's growth throughout the nineteenth and twentieth centuries, from Beethoven's sym-phonies to Stravinsky's ballets. In rehearsals, it's easier to listen to one voice than to attempt true musical democracy by listening to every musician, given the thousands of decisions required in any symphony, concerto or opera.

The first recorded baton-wielder in history was the Maestra of San Vito in Italy, who in 1594 led the nuns of the convent with a 'long, slender and well-polished wand . . . beating the measure of the time which they must obey in singing and playing'. Her indirect legacy became all too authoritative and all too male in the centuries that followed, as the image of the conductor controlling massed forces became an image of autocratic power. Elias Canetti, in his book *Crowds and Power*, calls the conductor the ideal tyrant: 'He is the living embodiment of law, both positive and negative. His hands decree and prohibit. His ears search out profanation.'

Yet the examples below tell another story: not of power wielded, but of a collectively created culture of listening, conveying an image not of perfected dictatorship, but of a give-and-take in which the individual musicians, and the conductor, are indivisible parts of a musical whole.

Jean-Baptiste Lully (1632–87)

Lully is the first musician to die of a conducting injury. Banging time on the floor with a conducting staff – effectively another percussion instrument in the orchestra – Lully hit his foot with an especially aggressive downbeat, conducting a *Te Deum* for the Sun King. Gangrene set in, and this great composer was gone thanks to conducting hubris.

Richard Wagner (1813–83)

By the nineteenth century, Wagner's hubris didn't involve staffs on the ground, but batons carving the air. The arrogance of Wagner's treatise On Conducting was all about putting his interpretations alongside and above the composer's notes. Wagner said that only he had the key to understanding Mozart or Beethoven, making the conductor essential as never before in musical culture.

Carlos Kleiber (1930–2004)

It's not only the sheer beauty of Kleiber's gestures in the air that are a transcendence of the weird arts of the conductor, it's how hard he worked to give his performances a unique intensity of feeling. The paradox is that Kleiber's concerts of Strauss, Mozart or Beethoven feel like improvisations, as if the music were being composed in the moment.

Claudio Abbado (1933–2014)

The last decade of Abbado's life was dominated by his work with the Lucerne Festival Orchestra. In a cycle of Mahler symphonies, he and his musicians achieved an exquisite symbiosis of listening. It was orchestral music played with the finesse of chamber music, a fierce sensitivity that sears through the films and recordings they made.

Mirga Gražinytė-Tyla (1986–)

Music Director of the City of Birmingham Symphony Orchestra from 2016 to 2022, Mirga Gražinytė-Tyla is a willing collaborator but uncompromising artistic leader, who has fearlessly explored unfamiliar repertoire – especially symphonies by Mieczysław Weinberg – and made the core repertoire her own, so that Beethoven and Stravinsky speak for her time, and ours.

41

The bells, the bells . . .

It's one of the most familiar sounds in all of our musical lives: the pealing or tolling of bells across a landscape or city scene; or the nightly rituals of Big Ben on the radio – each day ever so slightly different in rhythm, tone, and precise time, thanks to the effects of London's ever-changing atmosphere on the cracked bell that was installed in the tower of the Palace of Westminster in 1859. There are joyful bells that ring out in celebration of weddings, births or victories, and alarm bells that chime to warn of danger, or fall silent in times of war. So why is their clangorous magic still so powerful for us? Why do we respond so instinctively to bells – as sound, as idea, as symbol, as catalyst of musical and compositional possibility?

In music, it's not only Tchaikovsky who makes a bell-festooned racket, at the end of his *1812* overture, Stravinsky creates a whole piece that makes a synthetic ensemble of bells in *Les Noces*. Mike Oldfield's *Tubular Bells* is the uncannily reverberant music used in William Peter Blatty's movie *The Exorcist*; and there are Pierre Boulez's equally surreal electronic bells in *Répons*. Bells are also the inspiration behind Arvo Pärt's instantly recognisable 'tintinnabulation', the compositional technique that he found in the 1970s, derived from tinkling *tintinnabuli* – the Latin word for 'bells'.

In Britain, the artful science of the ringing of church bells operates according to extraordinarily long sequences of peals, or changes, that vary according to how many bells are in the tower. It's a remarkable fusion of mathematics, pattern-making and music, as the bells ring out their quarter-peal Bobs with their Sallys and Baldricks. If your church tower has six bells, to ring a full peal in any pattern would mean going through 720 permutations. If you have seven, that number grows exponentially to 5,040; with eight bells, there will be 40,320 different orderings that you would need for a complete peal. That feat of a complete eight-bell peal has only been accomplished once, by a Loughborough bell team in 1963, taking twenty-two hours to complete. And you thought Wagner's *Ring* cycle was epic – a true bell-ring cycle is much longer.

The question for composers is: how to deal with the raw sound of the bell? It's one of the richest sounds in the musical universe, because bell sounds are made from a vastly complex constellation of overtones that orbit a fundamental note.

In 1980, the British composer Jonathan Harvey made a piece of music based on bells, which sounds out a region between life and death. He took recordings of the singing of his son, who was then a boy chorister at Winchester Cathedral, and of the chiming of the cathedral's tenor bell. The piece is called *Mortuos Plango, Vivos Voco*, taken from an inscription written around the Winchester bell: 'I lament the dead, I call the living.' The piece transfuses the sounds in and out of each other, such that the bell seems to sing, and the boy's voice to chime. Harvey found 'curiously thrilling and disturbing' sounds in the complex halo of overtones this particular instrument produces: tones that don't conform to the conventional scales of Western music, and which are sounding mysteries that are still to be solved.

Then as now, bells sound out a region between and beyond; they are messengers that call us to a place between body and spirit, substance and shadow, life and loss.

◀ Ralph Vaughan Williams: Symphony no. 8 in D minor, fourth movement, 'Toccata'
◀ Pierre Boulez: *Répons*
◀ Igor Stravinsky: *Les Noces*
◀ Arvo Pärt: *Cantus in memoriam Benjamin Britten*
◀ Jonathan Harvey: *Mortuos Plango, Vivos Voco*

42

What makes the organ so mighty?

The organ: the biggest instrument ever created by human-kind, in structure, complexity, scale, and volume, played by musicians who are poly-limbed virtuosos of time and space, using their fingers at multiple keyboards, their feet on the pedal-boards. Organists control whole universes of colour, volume and intensity in every volley of chords, and in every spirit divine and demonic they invoke in their performances, from the power of Johann Sebastian Bach to Anna von Hauswolff, from Virgil Fox to Rick Wakeman. In cathedrals, concert halls and stadiums, the organ still reigns supreme: it is, as Mozart called it, 'the king of instruments'.

The biggest fully functioning organ on earth is in Macy's (formerly Wanamaker's) department store in Philadelphia. It's seven storeys high, with twenty-eight and a half thousand pipes, a building-sized organ in service of the God of Mammon. But it's a spiritual divinity that the organ so often symbolises, as an awesome musical creation that both realises humankind's sovereignty over the elements of acoustics and architecture, and invokes feelings of humility in the face of its sheer power. That's why the organ is so central for the religious music of Christian traditions.

In the eighteenth century, Johann Sebastian Bach's organ

works were part of the liturgical life of the churches he played in. His pieces are often written-down improvisations, compositions that turn the principles of his faith into musical material in flights of ecstatic intensity, like his most famous – still *the* most famous – work for organ, his Toccata and Fugue in D minor. The piece is a tribute to the power of the organ to render speechless any congregation who might hear it, in which the teenage Bach revels in his own powers as a firebrand musician, unleashing the sound and fury of the Toccata and the frenzied contrapuntal complexity of the Fugue. Nowadays, the Toccata and Fugue is associated as much with the dark side in popular culture as it is with the sounds of the divine: it's often a caped vampiric presence who offers up this music as a prelude to terror in a campy, Hammer-horror version of cinematic thrills and chills, and it's been covered by heavy metal bands as well as loftily austere organists.

Those associations with the dark side aren't as wacky as they seem. There's a sublime terror built into this music. Imagine walking into a church in 1705 while this music is playing, the organist unseen, the candlelight, cloaked figures huddling around the pillars, a preacher preparing a sermon of fire and brimstone, and the sounds of sublime sonic sulphur in Bach's music.

That association of the power of the organ with the extremities of spiritual experience, and sonic excess radiates through nineteenth-century traditions in the music of composers and improvisers like Anton Bruckner and Charles-Marie Widor, and continues in in the twentieth century in the work of another composer-organist – Olivier Messiaen, whose music takes the organ's delirium of feeling into still vaster dimensions.

In the twenty-first century, there's still a special quality of experience that these gigantic, consoling, sublime, multi-dimensional instruments uniquely access. The 'king of instruments' turns us all into royalty when we're hearing its astounding, earth-shattering sounds. We are all its subjects, blessed to live under the gaze of an instrument that's reigned for more than 2,000 years – and counting.

◀ Olivier Messiaen: *L'Ascension*
◀ Anna von Hauswolff: *Ceremony*
◀ Johann Sebastian Bach: Fantasia and Fugue in G minor, BWV 542 (Virgil Fox)
◀ Procol Harum: 'A Whiter Shade of Pale'
◀ Camille Saint-Saëns: Symphony no. 3 in C minor, 'Organ'

43

The synthesiser

Synthesisers and their precursors have been singing the body electric for decades: from keyboard synths in 1980s pop music back to the ethereal wails of the Theremin in the 1920s, or the ecstatic whoops of the Ondes Martenot in Olivier Messiaen's 1948 *Turangalîla* Symphony. The gates of musical perception that synthesisers have inspired musicians to fling open are summed up by Peter Zinovieff, one of the post-war synthesiser pioneers: 'Think of a sound – now make it.' That's the fundamentally utopian idea that drives synthesisers of the past, the present, and the future.

Musicians and inventors dreamt electrically as soon as they could. At the start of the twentieth century, the Italian futurists like Filippo Marinetti dreamt of electrically generated soundscapes as the logical outcome of music's acceptance of the modern world. The technology of the time was decades behind their ideas, as it was for Ferruccio Busoni, another Italian composer who was simultaneously a vigorous classicist and avant-garde theorist-dreamer. Instead it took the Theremin – patented by Leon Theremin in 1928 – to make electronic music a physical reality. The Theremin's sounds are made through the apparently telekinetic power of the musician's hands, moulding the air around an electrically charged wand: music is magicked out of the ether.

In the 1930s in Germany there was the Trautonium, a ribbon-based electronic instrument: you would slide your finger up and down the ribbon to control the pitch, manipulating other sonic parameters with dials underneath. Concertos for Trautonium and orchestra were composed by Harald Genzmer and Paul Hindemith, in which the synthetic future-sounds of the Trautonium are forced into a stiflingly neo-classical soundworld that seems far too polite for the instrument's alien invasion. And there's the Trautonium's cousin, the Ondes Martenot, invented in France in 1928, which was so beloved of Messiaen. His first piece for the Ondes was for no fewer than six of them, his *Fêtes des belles eaux* from 1937.

All these instruments have sonic glories – and technological compromises, because they couldn't use the full power of synthesis. They were making a tone and manipulating it according to only a handful of parameters, rather than giving the performer sculptural, creative power over a whole realm of new sounds.

That ability to dream in completely new sounds was what Peter Zinovieff wanted to make happen, and that's what he came up with in 1969 with his invention of the first commercially available synthesiser, the VCS3. There was no keyboard, but rather an elegant wooden box that housed a jauntily trapezoidal console with a joystick and a baroque explosion of knobs and controllers. The VCS3 was the progenitor of every synthesiser made ever since, from the Minimoog to the Yamaha DX7 and Korg M1, synths that dominated decades of pop music, and made their way into contemporary orchestras.

Today, software that's easily available on your laptop or smartphone allows you to realise Zinovieff's utopian dreams without leaving your sofa, but those earlier synthesisers are phenomena of the past that will always dream of the future, as they're used in new contexts and in new ways. It's a cliché to say that science fiction tells us more about the time it was written than it does about how things might be in the future. That's true of our relationship with synths too: they are visions of the future that are really about our present. We are all stardust – and synths are sonic stardust, too.

- ◀ Hannah Peel: 'Life Is on the Horizon'
- ◀ Gary Numan: 'Cars', from *The Pleasure Principle*
- ◀ Harold Faltermeyer: 'Axel F', theme tune to *Beverly Hills Cop*
- ◀ Paul Hindemith: *Konzertstück* for Trautonium and strings
- ◀ Kraftwerk: *Autobahn*

44

Virtuosity

We have now heard him, the strange wonder, whom the superstition of past ages, possessed by the delusion that such things could never have been done without the help of the Evil One, would undoubtedly have condemned to the stake . . . Just look at the pale, slender youth . . . those features so strongly stamped and full of meaning, in this respect reminding one of Paganini, who, indeed, has been his model of hitherto undreamt-of virtuosity and technical brilliance from the very first moment he heard him and was swept away.

That's the *Allgemeine musikalische Zeitung* on the pianist and composer Franz Liszt in 1838: but it could have been talking about preternaturally talented performers from across the centuries, virtuosos across musical genres, from the violinist Niccolò Paganini to the blues guitarist Robert Johnson, from the guitarist Berit Hagen – a.k.a. The Commander-in-Chief – to another guitar-shredding virtuoso, Eddie Van Halen. Because those virtuosos across musical times and places share not only a command of technique, rhetoric and performative brilliance, but also a critical and popular association with supernatural forces, as if their gifts were the result of some kind of diabolical possession.

And yet the real *diablerie* in the life-stories of these virtuosos isn't really in their deals with Mephistopheles: Robert Johnson didn't actually meet the Devil in the pale moonlight at a crossroads in Mississippi in order to become the greatest blues guitarist the world had ever known, as the legend goes – but we, his audiences, almost want to believe that he did. That's the truly diabolical phenomenon: why we, their listeners and spectators, want our virtuosos to come from the dark side. We want to be thrilled, titillated, disturbed and even afraid of their magical musical powers.

And after the nineteenth century's obsession with the diabolical frenzy that virtuosos like Liszt and Paganini could produce in their audiences, the place where the ideologies of the virtuoso are most powerful in the twentieth and twenty-first centuries is in blues, rock and heavy metal, especially among guitarists. They share a repertoire, too, because from the late 1960s, rock and early metal guitarists were drawn to classical music – especially the baroque, and especially Bach and Vivaldi – as proof of the brilliance of their technical prowess. Eddie Van Halen's 'Eruption', from 1978, is one of the moments that consecrates the electric guitar as a virtuosic instrument, and it's music that draws directly from the virtuosities of violin pedagogy – specifically, the Étude no. 5 by Rodolphe Kreutzer – to make its spectacular display. As Robert Walser puts it in his book about heavy metal's virtuosity, *Running with the Devil*, this solo 'is one minute and 27 seconds of exuberant and playful virtuosity, a violinist's precise and showy technique inflected by the vocal rhetoric of the blues and rock and roll irreverence'.

And where Eddie Van Halen led, hundreds of other rock and metal guitarists have followed, from Randy Rhoads to Yngwie Malmsteen, from Sebastian Bach to Berit Hagen, who has turned classical metal crossover into a career as The Commander-In-Chief.

So why do we listeners need virtuosos as entertainment and as transcendental musical nourishment for our culture – even for our souls? Because they create a bridge from their world of hyper-achievement to ours: through sensation and wonder they allow us, their listeners, to feel as superhuman as their musical powers make them. It's a trick, of course; an illusion produced by terrifying dedication and hard work – and practice. The devil, as always, is in the detail.

◀ Franz Liszt: *Mephisto Waltz* no. 1
◀ Robert Johnson: 'Cross Road Blues'
◀ Niccolò Paganini: *Caprice* in E major, op. 1 no. 1
◀ Eddie Van Halen: 'Eruption'
◀ The Commander-In-Chief (Berit Hagen): 'Thou', from *I Am*

45

Listening to recordings

How has sound recording changed our world? Whether we're part of the vinyl re-revolution, or streaming our music online, we live our lives through a haze of mechanically and digitally reproduced music. We're a long way from the phonautograph, the graphical picture of the sound-waves of the French folk song 'Au clair de la lune', made in 1860, or Ludwig Koch's recording of his pet bird from 1889, when the budding sound recordist was just eight years old.

In the early twentieth century, Enrico Caruso became synonymous with the phonograph, the embodiment – or rather, the disembodiment – of the possibilities of the medium. His voice transfixed millions, and his records motivated bourgeois households all over the world to equip themselves with the vast furniture of the early gramophones. Caruso's records were miraculous fetish objects. These discs, made from the backs of beetles in their shiny shellac, consecrated technology's victory over time. Music, otherwise in the ether, was captured, stored, and replayable: Caruso's voice and Puccini's melodies were yours, in your hands, playing for you whenever you desired.

What creative musicians quickly started to realise was that recording wasn't only a reproductive tool – it was a new medium, a new art-form in itself. Instead of pretending that it could replicate music out there in the wild, it was much better to use recording technologies for what they could do differently. The gap between a recording and the real-life acoustic experience opened up a whole new field of phonography that musicians, producers and sound-artists have been exploring ever since.

By the 1950s and 60s, the studio itself was an instrument, from the surreal acoustic dreams of The Beach Boys and The Beatles to the aural cinema of the producer John Culshaw's recording of Wagner's *Ring* cycle, with the Vienna Philharmonic conducted by Georg Solti. But music's journey with these magical, time-transcending objects – LPs, vinyl, tape – had a further stage to go through in the late 1970s and 80s: from an analogue world of sound-waves being recorded and amplified, to the digital world of CDs, in which sounds become information. John Cage said that music was all around us, all we had to do was tune in to it. That's now literally true: it's not just the radio – over the internet, music has been atomised and etherealised. 150 years on from the very start of the story of sound recording, music is again written on the air. But now, we can capture all of it, all the time.

And yet for me, the most magical manifestation of sound recording's power to create permanence out of the impermanence of sound-waves comes from 1977, and it's very definitely an object: Carl Sagan's Golden Record, sent up with the Voyager spacecraft on its infinite interstellar mission, providing the tools for any passing alien civilisations to reproduce music from Chuck Berry to J. S. Bach, and a chorus of human voices and languages. As Sagan himself said: 'Billions of years from now, our sun . . . will have reduced Earth to a charred cinder. But the Voyager record will still be largely intact . . . preserving a murmur of an ancient civilisation that once flourished . . . on the distant planet Earth.'

- ◀ Karlheinz Stockhausen: *Kontakte*
- ◀ Frank Ocean: 'Close to You', from *Blonde*
- ◀ James Reese Europe: 'On Patrol in No Man's Land' (Lieut. Jim Europe's 369th Infantry 'Hell Fighters' Band)
- ◀ The Beach Boys: 'Heroes and Villains', from *Smiley Smile*
- ◀ Kate Bush: 'The Sensual World'

46

Technology

The medium is the message, and the message is: technology matters, because without crystal sets and valves, microphones and headphones and wirelesses and multiple linked satellites, none of the things we call radio or recorded music would be possible. We are all enmeshed in the network: we are the musical matrix.

And it's not only in how we receive it: music is dependent on technology at every stage of its creation, production and reception. No technology would mean no organs, no pianos, harpsichords or synthesisers. And that's just to take one family of instruments: the same is true for all of them, in the metal- and wood- and reed-working of the woodwinds, in the twists and turns of all that brass in trumpets and French horns; or the architectural science and building techniques that make our concert halls, from eighteenth-century living rooms to nineteenth-century musical marquees like the Royal Albert Hall, to gleaming twentieth- and twenty-first-century auditoria of glass, concrete and steel.

So are all these technologies the result of scientific exploration to further the boundaries of sound, or do they exist because the horizons of sonic possibility had to be made ever wider for composers to realise their musical dreams? The answer is – both, in the creative dance between music and technological development over the centuries.

Richard Wagner asked for a new instrument for his *Ring* cycle, something between the horn and the trombone – which was exactly what was made for him, and the Wagner tuba was born. In the twentieth century, the Italian visionary Ferruccio Busoni dreamt of new scales and new instruments, and Edgard Varèse asked questions that the technology of the 1950s couldn't answer when he was making his electronic music. In the 1960s, Peter Zinovieff wanted 'every nun to have a Synthi', as he advertised his new instrument, to access the world of synthesised sounds. And Daphne Oram at the BBC Radiophonic Workshop came up with new ways of writing and hearing music, and also made her Oramics machine, which allowed you to draw on 35mm film, shapes that would be translated into electronic sounds. Oram wanted everyone to experience the immediacy of electronic-musical creation, to have an intimate relationship with our own worlds of sound.

But pushing the limits of technology is what Ludwig van Beethoven was doing too, when he wrote pitches in his pieces that the pianos of the early nineteenth century simply couldn't play – they didn't have enough notes. And as a species, we've always been remaking our sonic world, from the time we started pounding the walls of our caves a hundred thousand years ago to create the first lithophones (stone instruments); or when we refashioned griffon bones into flutes. This primordial music technology was an act of imagination as well as an exploration of the physics of sound.

Whatever we're listening to, we're never hearing one thing separate from the other, the technological apart from the musical. They are always together: music is the sound of technology; technology is a catalyst for musical creation.

And today, what happens to our digital selves, as our information is turned into sound-bytes for eternity? We are all information-age sound and stardust in the twenty-first century. In the creative entanglement of music and technology, we sing the soul electric.

- ◀ Daphne Oram: *Brociliande*
- ◀ Daniel Bedingfield: 'Gotta Get Thru This'
- ◀ Ludwig van Beethoven: Piano Sonata no. 29 in B flat major, op. 126, 'Hammerklavier'
- ◀ Wendy Carlos: 'Beethoviana', from the soundtrack to *A Clockwork Orange*
- ◀ Pierre Schaeffer: *Cinq études de bruits*, no. 1, 'Étude aux chemins de fer'

47

How does video game music work?

What's the most significant new dimension added to the interactive possibilities of music in recent history? It's been happening since the late 1970s: music for video games.

It's no accident that we use the same adjective for what we do with music and what we do with video games: we play them. And the connections go deeper than we think, in terms of what it feels like to play music and to play games, whether it's *Super Mario Bros.* or *Halo*, the *Final Fantasy* series or *The Legend of Zelda*. One of the designers of what's considered one of the greatest games ever made, Nintendo's *Super Mario Galaxy*, compares the prestidigitatory skills of running and jumping and power-up-collecting that players develop as they progress through the levels to learning a musical instrument. Just as playing the piano is more fulfilling the more skilled you are, the pleasure of the game increases as you improve how you control Mario, that short, rotund, moustachioed plumber, who has bestridden the world of gaming as an unlikely colossus for more than thirty-five years.

But the idea of 'playing' is more profound than virtuosic up-skilling. When we play music, or when we're taken over by it when we're listening, we feel that we're part of the piece. The sounds couldn't happen without us if we're playing or singing, and if we're really listening, we can have a ventriloquising sensation that the music couldn't happen without our participation in it. We are agents of the way the music happens.

And it's that agency that video games give us in a way that no other medium can. That immersion isn't only made with our eyes, it's made with our ears. The soundworlds of video games are what truly draws us into their imaginative constructs of science-fiction dystopias or medieval fantasy worlds. And thanks to the way that video-game music so often works, when we're given this magical agency of controlling the avatars we see on the screen, we also become composers of the sounds we hear. The sequence of sounds you hear in a game is dependent on how you play the level, which in-game villages you visit, or how often your character dies – very often indeed if you're as bad at *Super Mario 3D Land* as I am – meaning that we're effectively composing our way through these games, playing their music, and being played by their music, as well as their game-worlds.

Composers writing video-game music are multi-dimensional musical creators who give us creative agency, as we compose our way through the labyrinths of their imaginations, and the worlds the game designers create for us. Video games need us, their players, just as music needs us, its listeners. And in our interactions with video-game music, our listening becomes world-creating participation.

◀ Koji Kondo: suite from *The Legend of Zelda*
◀ Nobuo Uematsu: theme from *Final Fantasy VII*
◀ Jessica Curry: score for *Everybody's Gone to the Rapture*
◀ Jesper Kyd: *Hitman: Blood Money*
◀ Garry Schyman: 'The Ocean on his Shoulders', from *Bioshock*

48

Extreme voices

We all have voices: we speak with them, we scream and shout and whisper with them; we murmur, prattle and hum; we ululate and rap and belt and twang and sing. But some vocal extremophiles can go beyond even those vocal realities: some voices can simultaneously sing two, or even three lines of over-tones; others can create undertones of growling noise, like the grindcore band Napalm Death, or create symphonies from screams, like Diamanda Galás.

The outer edges of what's vocally possible are a resource that composers have called on, just as musicians have pushed themselves to their limits. Mozart composed the stratospheric soprano part of the Queen of the Night in *The Magic Flute* for his sister-in-law, Josepha Hofer. And those top Fs in her Act 2 aria 'Der Hölle Rache', surfing the leger lines way above the top of the treble clef, have an equally extreme expressive function. They aren't merely decorative musical baubles, but an exquisitely vicious arpeggiation, as the Queen of the Night commands her daughter Pamina to murder Sarastro. Those top Fs cut like an assassin's knife.

There are many more extreme divas of the screaming stratosphere in our musical lives: from Björk to Kate Bush to Minnie Riperton. For male voices, there's a different extreme

– how low can they go? One answer is the vocal abyss at the end of the 'Nunc Dimittis' from Rachmaninoff's Vespers. The basses reach down to a low B flat, below the edges of the bass clef. And something weird happens when we hear this music: it's as if the bass-line starts to float, the lower it gets. Instead of the sound seeming to get heavier, as you might think would happen the further down you go, Rachmaninoff makes these notes hover, suspending us over the abyss.

It's axiomatic that when you sing, you're singing one line, one musical texture. We can't sing more than one note, can we? Well yes, we can! The Tuvan and Mongolian traditions of throat singing achieve effects of up to three different overtones and undertones chiming around a single fundamental note. This music is the sound of human voices creating the illusion of whole eco-systems of savannah and birdsong, of wild horses and keening prayers and laments.

But for the ultimate in vocal extremity, the acme of human-produced sonic scintillation, the last word in the virtuosity of the voice, all you have to do it listen to – yourself. In our exultations of delight and laughter, our moments of ecstasy and horror, our exclamations of joy and pain, we are all giving voice to our own unique expressions of – everything we're capable of as human beings. And no one else can do it quite the way you can: yours is an absolutely individual instrument, as distinctive and as perfectly calibrated to who you are as Diamanda Galás's voice, or Björk's, as individual and as complete in your expression as operatic sopranos or Mongolian throat singers. We're all vocal extremists: and we're doing it every day, every time we open our mouths.

- ◀ Alash: 'My Throat, the Cuckoo', from *Achai*
- ◀ Björk: 'Triumph of a Heart', from *Medúlla*
- ◀ Diamanda Galás: 'Wild Women with Steak Knives', from *The Litanies of Satan*
- ◀ Sergei Rachmaninoff: 'Nunc Dimittis', from *Vespers*
- ◀ Napalm Death: 'Silence is Deafening', from *The Code Is Red...Long Live the Code*

49

How to sing classical – vibrato!

Vibrato. The tremulous vibration that opera singers and classically trained voices produce. But what really is the wobble? Is it the artifice of classical singing or is it a naturally occurring phenomenon in the physicality of our vocal cords, in the way our larynxes make the sounds we call singing?

There's evidence across the whole of musical culture that vibrato is far from being only a cliché of the classical. In fact, vibrato is everywhere there are voices: from Iron Maiden's Bruce Dickinson to Whitney Houston, from Bulgarian women's choirs to Bollywood, Japanese Noh Theatre to Broadway shows.

But there are as many types of vibrato as there are singers, and the difference between a controlled vibration and an uncontrolled wobble is the difference between taste – good and bad – across musical genres, whatever their starting standards of vibrato. But what is it, physically, sonically speaking? If vibrato is a change of pitch, so that the note goes up and down in frequency, how much are you allowed to change the note before it becomes something else, a trill between different notes, or an out-of-control oscillation? How fast or slow should the rate of vibration in vibrato be?

Mozart said his ideal was a vibration of around six times a second, and the greatest singers, in whatever tradition they come from, use a continuum from minimal wobble to maximum oscillation for the greatest possible expressive effect. Billie Holiday is a virtuoso of microscopically rich vocal control in her performance of 'I'll Be Seeing You'. On the first note of the song, she starts with no vibrato at all, but she warms the sounds up towards the end of the note so that it ends in a halo of pure vibration. Her vibrato isn't employed to fill a vast auditorium, as opera singers use it, but to make our souls shake with empathy through the way she plays with the intimacy of the microphone. Holiday's voice plays with our heartstrings, and her vibrato – which she can turn into a shimmer of vibration at the end of the note, so all we hear is the vibrating air, not the note itself – is an echo of pure sympathy with the longing of this lyric and this voice.

Vibrato is what makes our human singing human. It's the inner dynamism of any vocal sound, and our own particular vibrato is the individual signature of our vocal cords, of our unique voices. Without these variously microscopic tremulations or macroscopic wobbles, we would all sing like T-Pain or Cher after they've been put through the technological mixer: singers who have the vibrato shorn off their voices to make the very particular but dehumanising effect that Auto-tune software has on real voices. Instead, when we glory in Maria Callas or Luciano Pavarotti, Ian Bostridge or Anna Netrebko, Billie Holiday or Whitney Houston, we feel our bodies resonate in sympathy with the sounds they make and the feelings they inspire. Without vibrato, without that inner, ever-changing life of their vocal sounds, our hearts would run cold rather than overflowing with feeling: no vibrato, no life.

- Whitney Houston: 'I Will Always Love You' (Dolly Parton)
- Vincenzo Bellini: 'Casta diva', from *Norma* (Maria Callas, Orchestra of La Scala Milan, Tullio Serafin)
- Cher: 'Believe' (Paul Michael Barry)
- Europe: 'The Final Countdown' (Joey Tempest)
- Billie Holiday: 'I'll Be Seeing You' (Sammy Fain/ Irving Kahal)

50

Countertenors – classical rock gods!

Alfred Deller, James Bowman, Jeff Buckley, Frankie Valli, Lawrence Zazzo, Jimmy Somerville, Tiny Tim and Smokey Robinson: countertenors, one and all, voices who explore regions that most of us hardly dare to imagine, let alone to inhabit.

How do they do it? How do their voices get up there? You can hear the answer when you listen to the Gibb brothers in the Bee Gees. If you sing along to 'How Deep is Your Love?' and you happen to be an adult male, you're going to have use something that's called falsetto: it's a subtly different way of using the voice that allows Robin Gibb – and classical countertenors like Iestyn Davies or Lawrence Zazzo – to get up into the stratosphere. The sound is often less vibrato-laden, so it's less wobbly, and it's a miraculous register that all of us can find above the range of the voice we usually use. You can get there by swooping up the whole length of your vocal range, and finding the point at which your voice seems to break out into a higher set of notes: that's where your very own 'falsetto' begins.

But that apparently simple word, 'falsetto', is a clue to the disruptive power that countertenors have in musical culture: the way they force us to rethink categories of voice types, of what it is that men's and women's voices are supposed to sound like, and the way they liquefy some of the boundaries between them. It's that word 'falsetto', which means 'false voice' in Italian. That suggests there's something not quite real about singers who use this voice. These ideas are still so entrenched in classical culture that people can still react in shock to countertenors in concerts and opera houses, thinking 'Why is that man singing so high?', as if it were an affront to their perceptions of masculinity – and then go home and listen to falsettoing rockers like Smokey Robinson or countertenoring pop star like Justin Timberlake without batting an earlid.

Classical music's nuanced relationship with the countertenor voice type might have arisen because of the large body of vocal music in the seventeenth and eighteenth centuries composed for castrati: castrated male singers, the male sopranos for whom Handel composed so many roles. Castrati like Farinelli and Senesino were the rock gods of their time. Everyone knew that there were parts of their anatomy conventionally associated with maleness that were missing, but that only enhanced their on-stage performance of preening and priapic masculinity. Theirs was seen and heard as a stratospherically gendered performance – exactly as the highest registers in rock, metal and pop today are sounds of hyper-masculinity, from Jeff Buckley to Jon Bon Jovi, from James Brown to Pharrell Williams. It's not disturbing if you're a pop fan that men sing high, but in classical music, the countertenor can still surprise and shock by his mere existence.

Classical culture is catching up with the rest of the musical world – and with the roles played by countertenor voices in its own history. Countertenors are here to stay, just as they have been for most of the last half-millennium and more of musical history in the West. Theirs isn't an exotic vocal flavour, but a virtuosically normal voice type. The countertenor's future isn't as musical counter-culture, but as mainstream. And the possibilities have only just begun.

- ◀ George Frideric Handel: arias from *Serse* (Lawrence Zazzo, Vivica Genaux, Lautten Compagney)
- ◀ Antonio Vivaldi: *Nisi Dominus* (Andreas Scholl, Paul Dyer, Australian Brandenburg Orchestra)
- ◀ Bee Gees: 'Stayin' Alive', from *Saturday Night Fever*
- ◀ Philip Glass: *Akhnaten*
- ◀ James Brown: 'I Got You (I Feel Good)', from *Out of Sight*

Why backing vocals matter

Brian Eno had it right: all the world's problems, he said, can be solved 'with either oyster sauce or backing vocals'. He's especially right when it comes to the latter. Aretha Franklin's 'I Say a Little Prayer', The Mamas & the Papas' 'California Dreamin'', The Moody Blues' 'Nights in White Satin': it's the backing vocals that make the musical sauce in all those tracks. But it's not only in individual songs that the power of the backing vocal is at its most alchemical, it's in whole shows, musicals, operettas and operas.

So why, given how essential they are to rock, pop and opera stages, are backing singers and choruses so often taken for granted? The thinking of the French post-structuralist philosopher Jacques Derrida may help us understand the significance of the rest of the Beach Boys in relation to Brian Wilson, or of the opera chorus in relation to Donizetti's or Verdi's solo tenors. Derrida's notion of the 'supplement' suggests that the thing itself is incomplete without its supplement, so that the supplement is no sense optional, but, instead, fundamental.

That's the paradox of the chorus or the backing vocal group: imagine Gladys Knight and no Pips; Verdi's *Il trovatore* without the Anvil Chorus; or Mussorgsky's *Boris Godunov* without its choirs of revolting populace, or Queen's 'Somebody to Love' without the voices who aren't Freddie Mercury: not only would the music not be the same, it wouldn't be the thing itself at all. Instead of being in the background, choruses and backing singers are right there in the musical and philosophical centre-stage.

The symbiosis of a solo performer in dialogue with a larger group can be found in the original backing groups of theatrical history: the Greek choruses from the tragedies that played in their amphitheatres. Greek choruses were a bridge to our experience in the audience, connecting us to the tragedy, reminding us that none of us can escape the machinations of fate, the cruel games of the gods.

That convention of the chorus as Greek-style commentator is still in place in the late seventeenth century in Britain. Henry Purcell gives the chorus the same role in his opera *Dido and Aeneas*. Dido laments her demise, in one of the most famous pieces of music ever composed, but that descending, weeping, keening song of the abyss isn't the end of the opera. It's the chorus who have the final word: they're empathetic sounding boards for us in the audience, who interpret the events of the drama and communicate their world of myth to the audience. Dido's 'Remember me, but ah! Forget my fate' becomes a chorus of Cupids, singing:

> *With drooping wings you Cupids come,*
> *And scatter roses on her tomb.*
> *Soft and gentle as her heart*
> *Keep here your watch, and never part.*

So why, as Brian Eno says, are backing singers and opera choruses the solution to all musical and possibly social problems? Because they make a bridge of resonating, reverberating empathy from the song and the opera, through the community of singers to the audience. We admire and are awed by the soloists and the principals – but we're invited to join in, to feel, to move, to sing along, by the diamond-setting of all those backing singers. They make all of this music – from 'Midnight Train' to Mussorgsky – ours, as well as theirs.

◀ Aretha Franklin: 'I Say a Little Prayer', from
   Aretha Now
◀ Queen: 'Somebody to Love', from *A Day at the Races*
◀ Igor Stravinsky: *The Rake's Progress*
◀ Henry Purcell: *Dido and Aeneas*
◀ Gladys Knight & the Pips: 'Midnight Train to Georgia'
   (Jim Weatherly)

A CORNUCOPIA OF CURIOUS IDEAS

What is 'classical music'?

Here's a simple question: did Johann Sebastian Bach think he
was writing 'classical music'? Did Wolfgang Amadé Mozart?
Did Ludwig van Beethoven? No – they absolutely did not.
And yet we call them 'classical', in fact we've made them the
very acme of it. So what is it?

'Classical music' has at the very least become an effective
marketing term. Maybe you remember the classical sections in
record shops in the late twentieth century: always behind frosted
glass doors, sequestered away from other, noisier genres: *shhhh!*
Walk on tiptoes on the sound-absorbing carpets; whisper to the
attendant about the secrets of the latest releases of Harnoncourt,
Hewitt and Hough. We are classical – we are very quiet, and we
exist in our own world of meditative perfection . . .

That's one of the ongoing crimes of the 'classical music'
racket: in removing the music to some other place of quasi-
religious reverence, the term swaddles and suffocates the viv-
idness, danger and violence of the music it supposedly defines.

When was the term 'classical music' first coined? In English, we have a reasonably precise moment when the label first
appeared in print: in 1829, in Vincent and Mary Novello's *A
Mozart Pilgrimage*, when they talk of a 'place I should come to
every Sunday when I wished to hear classical music correctly

and judiciously performed'. But there's a lot of cultural work between the use of this label in this specific Mozartian context and its blob-like colonisation of so much music composed between roughly AD 1000 and the present day, from Hildegard von Bingen to Judith Weir – not to mention everything from film soundtracks to avant-garde classics.

The seduction of the idea of 'classical music' is that it emerges at a time in the nineteenth century when the European bourgeoisie began to congregate in halls and auditoria built for the express purpose of making an aspirational middle class feel jolly good about itself.

And yet this has nothing to do with the sounds and ideals of the music subsumed under this label. Even the music of the 'classical period' – another misnomer, a retrospective definition of music composed between 1750 and, roughly, 1800 – only embodies the eternal virtues of the 'classical' if we turn our ears and imaginations away from the expressive intensity of what composers like Joseph Haydn and Mozart were really doing. Which was shaking us up, not writing soundtracks for concert-hall mausoleums of bourgeois self-congratulation.

And yet: the fact that the music encompassed by the term 'classical music' now has more range, musically and historically, and less specificity than pretty well any other generic category, is arguably its strength. The confusion, the diversity, the open-endedness, means that those glass doors that used to separate the 'classical' from the rest of the musical universe have been shattered.

Instead of being stumped by not being able to define it, maybe we should just relax: the 'classical' is now everywhere, from games to soundtracks, from concert halls to playlists. It's broken out of the hermetically sealed glass box – and it's not going back. And thank goodness for that.

◀ Wolfgang Amadé Mozart: Symphony no. 40 in G minor, K550, first movement
◀ Ludovico Einaudi: *Le Onde*
◀ Judith Weir: Piano Concerto
◀ William Walton: *Façade*
◀ Hildegard von Bingen: *O vis aeternitatis*

53

Whatever happened to the waltz?

Dance has always been a danger to European social propriety. In sixteenth-century England, the court of Queen Elizabeth I danced a precursor of the waltz, the volta – like the waltz, a triple-time dance of pleasure. As Johannes Praetorius described it in *The Practices of Witchcraft*: 'The volta is full of scandalous, beastly gestures and immodest movements . . . innumerable murders and miscarriages are brought about by it.' Dancing, and especially dances with that pleasurable excess of a third beat – instead of being tied to the one–two mundanity of marches, the waltz and the volta fly free with that extra beat in the bar – could bring about social and moral collapse.

Nineteenth-century Vienna was the epicentre of a continent's obsession with the waltz. With music composed by the waltz kings, the Strausses, its waltz-mania was consecrated in dance-halls like the Sperl, with its Winter Garden – so large you couldn't see one end from the other – and the Apollo, which had live swans and a fake waterfall. These waltz-palaces were even equipped with birthing rooms so that pregnant mothers wouldn't miss the next dance. Johann Strauss II presided over these mythical places, writing music that trapped his dancers in chains of pleasure, with dreams of the Blue Danube and the

Roses of the South. *The Blue Danube* isn't only a waltz – it's a tone-poem of nostalgia, and Strauss's endless melodies are so good that Brahms wished he had written them.

So much pleasure, so much dancing on the edge of the volcano of Europe's political turmoil. The waltz era couldn't last. The First World War sounded the death-knell of the waltz-palaces, and we're still suspicious of all those ballrooms and all that gilded excess more than a century after the fall of the Hapsburg Empire. The pianist Ricardo Viñes described this precipice of pleasure, after going to the Opera Ball in Paris in 1905 with the composer Maurice Ravel: 'As always when I see young beautiful women, lights and all this activity, I thought of death, of the ephemeral nature of everything. I imagined balls from past generations who are now nothing but dust, as will be all the masks I saw, and in a short while! What horror. Oblivion!'

Ravel mixed that visionary memory of waltzing terror with his wartime experiences in *La Valse*, composed in 1920, in which the waltz rhythm is progressively annihilated by his orchestration. *La Valse* is the sound of the volcano under the nineteenth-century waltz erupting.

Later in the twentieth century, Leonard Cohen wrote his song 'Take this Waltz', another hymn to the waltz's exquisite, dangerous ambiguity: 'Take this waltz with the clamp on its jaws . . . Take this waltz – it's been dying for years.' The waltz: the sound and the sensation of pleasure curdling deliciously into pain, loss and nostalgia, a siren song that we still can't resist.

- ◀ Johann Strauss II: *The Blue Danube*
- ◀ Hector Berlioz: *Symphonie fantastique*, second movement, 'Un bal'
- ◀ Pyotr Ilyich Tchaikovsky: Symphony no. 6 in B minor, 'Pathétique', second movement
- ◀ Maurice Ravel: *La Valse*
- ◀ Leonard Cohen: 'Take This Waltz', from *I'm Your Man*

54

Prog rock – apotheosis or nadir?

Progressive – prog – rock: the utopian genre of musical exper-
imentation that has used, extended and transformed the repertoires of classical music, its sense of scale, its rhetoric and its
own ridiculous conventions and turned them all the way up to
eleven. And beyond.

A musician like Rick Wakeman shows how prog and classical
are intimately entwined with one another. Wakeman is a classically trained prog guru, and since the 1960s, he's been a seer of
new forms and styles that fuse together bands and batteries of
keyboards with orchestras. He has conceived albums like creative
Gesamtkunstwerks that rival anything the conjuror of Bayreuth
came up with in their genre-melting ambition. But Wakeman has
far outstripped Wagner in terms of the technology of his shows
with his band Yes, or his solo albums of meta-historical-mythic
keyboard virtuosity, or quasi-operatic concept-album concerts
like *Journey to the Centre of the Earth* or *King Arthur*. Wagner
never staged one of his mythic music dramas on ice – even if he
dreamt of putting on the *Ring* in the middle of a lake. But Rick
Wakeman went there, performing *King Arthur* in an ice-rink –
and in his trademark cape, too, glinting in all its sequinned glory
off the thousand lights above him as his octopus-like hands tore
into virtuosic solos like 'Merlin the Magician'.

Fusions of classical and prog repertoire run through albums made in the late 1960s and 70s: Emerson, Lake & Palmer re-made Ginastera, Mussorgsky, Copland, Tchaikovsky and Parry; Rick Wakeman did the same for Brahms; and King Crimson worked with Samuel Barber's music.

And if you look closely at the substance of prog rock's utopian visions, they resemble, in sound and substance, the ideals of classical music culture. Both have inspired the creation of vast structures and spectacles of theatre and sound that break conventions to communicate epic narratives of destruction and renewal. That's Yes, and Genesis, and ELP – and it's Wagner's *Ring* cycle and Karlheinz Stockhausen's seven *Licht* operas. Both classical and prog are also about the creation of a culture of listening as serious-minded as the music purports to be, a worshipful adoration of performers and composers as high priests of a quasi-religious transport of delight. And both share a clichéd public image of snobbishness curdling into kitsch, a self-conscious elitism in the face of more popular cultures, whether bubblegum three-minute songs or potboiling orchestral miniatures.

The prog instincts – to create transcendental experiences, and have an ecstatic time while you're doing it, whether you're making the music or listening to it – that's what classical music culture should be about too. Rick Wakeman has called for a Prog Prom at the Royal Albert Hall. It must happen!

◀ Emerson, Lake & Palmer: *Tarkus*
◀ King Crimson: 'The Court of the Crimson King'
◀ Genesis: 'Supper's Ready', from *Foxtrot*
◀ Rick Wakeman: 'Cans and Brahms', from *Fragile* (performed by Yes)
◀ Yes: 'The Revealing Science of God', from *Tales from Topographic Oceans*

55

Why is opera so ridiculous?

Opera: the greatest art-form on earth, the most elaborate, complex, fulfilling and ambitious multi-media creation of live performance that humankind has ever conceived. But there is another side to opera. Because there's a perilously fine line in operatic performance between the sublime and the ludicrous. No art-form shoots for the stars so ambitiously, and no other spectacle of human endeavour can also hit the bathetic lows of the ridiculous, the overblown and the unintentionally hilarious.

That's because no other art-form on Earth demands as much suspension of disbelief as opera. The singers in Act 3 of Wagner's *Tristan and Isolde* don't actually expire in a mystic union of their souls in the opera house. The tenor and the so-prano are playing characters who are supposedly both on the brink of death and some kind of transcendent spiritual-erotic communion, yet they're singing at the extremes of what the human voice can do. The glory of the music and the voices is a completely synthetic multi-media event, made from Wagner's words and music. And yet, this profound artificiality is exactly the mechanism that reveals a heightened operatic emotional truth.

You need the same suspension of disbelief across the whole of the operatic spectrum: at the end of Leoncavallo's *Pagliacci*

– about everyone's favourite murderous clown, apart from Pennywise in Stephen King's *It* – the characters sing outrageously sensual music as they're killing and dying, as human beings tend not to in real life. Mozart's *The Magic Flute* is a glorious mess of a pseudo-mystical plot which makes no objective sense, and yet when we see it on stage, we become willing participants in the fairy-tale, so that we revel in the fantastical melange of ideas, symbols and stories. They might not come together in any satisfying way as a plot yet the magic carpet of the music, and the staging, can make us believe that they do.

And that's when the alchemy of opera releases its deeper emotional truths. The way the voices of Nerone and Poppea intertwine with one another at the end of Claudio Monteverdi's *L'incoronazione di Poppea* is a sounding image of bodies and souls flowing together in timeless sensuality. The characters may have unleashed death and destruction on their world – but none of that matters in the sublime solipsism of their lust for one another. Monteverdi's music is the most gorgeous, the most amoral, and the most libidinously supercharged duet, as two bodies, and two voices, melt into one another in selfish, seductive oblivion in their final unison.

That's the point: we confront the white-heat of our emotions head-on in the opera house, without the need for anything so mundane as reality – or morality – getting in the way. 'Suspend your disbelief, all ye who enter here,' should be written above the entrance of every opera house on earth – they're magical machines for the transportation of our souls to new regions of delight.

- Richard Wagner: *Tristan and Isolde*
- Ruggero Leoncavallo: *Pagliacci*
- Wolfgang Amadé Mozart: *The Magic Flute*
- Claudio Monteverdi: *L'incoronazione di Poppea*
- Gerald Barry: *The Importance of Being Earnest*

Background music

Music you're not supposed to listen to – background music. There's a lot of it out there, from Muzak to ambient, from chill-out to elevator music: paradoxical genres of music that say: Don't listen to me! Keep shopping! Keep relaxing! Keep partying! Keep eating! But whatever you do, don't listen to this!

By putting the background in the foreground, you can find a history of background music that's longer than you might imagine: eighteenth-century composers like Mozart wrote countless hours of music for the background long before the Muzak corporation started pumping music into workplaces in America in the twentieth century.

Mozart wrote background music? His serenades, like *Eine kleine Nachtmusik*, his divertimenti, his dances, were composed as accompaniments to aristocratic social entertainments; to be appreciated, but not listened to closely. Before the French composer Erik Satie's 'furniture music', before Brian Eno's *Music for Airports*, eighteenth-century composers were writing background music.

Satie dreamt of his *Musique d'ameublement* in 1917, to function as an accompaniment to modern life. He wrote pieces with titles like 'Phonic Tiling – Can be played during a lunch or civil marriage – Movement: Ordinary'. But the only set of furniture pieces that were actually played in his lifetime were 'At a Bistro' and 'A Drawing Room', in the interval of a play by Max Jacob in 1920. The problem was that the musicians found they were being listened to in attentive silence rather than as background atmosphere, as Satie's weird, repetitive music – each piece is just a few bars long, to be repeated into the infinite – was performed. They had to tell their audience not to listen, but instead to get up and walk around, and talk to each other.

Where Satie failed, the Muzak Corporation succeeded, compiling albums in the mid-twentieth century in America called *Stimulus Progression*, whose elegant string arrangements and mid-tempo jazzisms were designed to mirror and amplify the rhythms of the working day when they were played in factories and shopping malls. Muzak worked, the corporation said, because 'when you employ the science of Muzak, in an office, workers tend to get more done, more efficiently, and feel happier. In an industrial plant, people feel better and, with less fatigue and tension, their jobs seem less monotonous.' Lyndon B. Johnson used Muzak in his White House, NASA's scientists plotted their course to the Moon under the influence of Muzak's albums.

And if we're honest with ourselves, so much of the listening we all do is when we have music on in the background. Few of us actually give our full attention in splendid isolation to the CD we've just bought or the album we're just streaming: life – your phone, the internet, your family, possibly not in that order – intervene in all the glorious, messy, and sound-ful ways that they do, so that's it's just easier to put John Coltrane on as you do the washing up, or a spot of Judith Weir as you make a well-earned coffee. From serenades to Music While

You Work, the background has been in the foreground, all along. Muzak and music – they're part of the same continuum.

◀ Wolfgang Amadé Mozart: *Eine kleine Nachtmusik*,
  K525, first movement
◀ Muzak: 'Paradise Program', from *Stimulus Progression 6*
◀ Brian Eno: *Music for Airports*
◀ Erik Satie: 'Chez un "bistrot"', from *Musique
  d'ameublement, 2 entr'actes*
◀ David Lewis Luong: 'Memoir of Summer', from
  Best of Elevator Music & Mall Music

57

Maxing out on minimalism

Minimalism, that most popular, most divisive and most misunderstood of all twentieth-century musical movements: the sounds of rhythmically repetitive music by a quartet of American composers, Reich, Glass, Young and Riley – Steve, Philip, La Monte and Terry respectively – who defined the movement, the style and the genre of minimalism in the 1960s and 70s. Take a chord, a rhythmic pattern, a handful of notes, and repeat them – and repeat again.

But repetitive pulsation is only one kind of minimalism, because there's also the drone-based music of Éliane Radigue and Pauline Oliveros. There are Michael Nyman's film scores, and given that Nyman was the first to actually use the phrase 'minimalist' to describe pieces of music in 1968, he should know how it's done. Let alone the minimalist techniques of rhythmic propulsion and harmonic monomania that have made their way into pop tunes and film soundtracks, from Mike Oldfield's *Tubular Bells* to the scores of Hans Zimmer.

Which all begs the question: just what is minimalism? It isn't so 'minimal' at all, if it can encompass all these musics, and other art-forms. Visual artists prefigure the work of musical minimalists by decades, from Kazimir Malevich's *Black Square*, from 1915, to Yves Klein's *Monotone Symphony*, from

1949: a single chord, to be played for twenty minutes, followed by twenty minutes of silence.

What connects all these composers and artists is a desire to change the parameters of how their art-form and the world around them is perceived. In music, it might seem ironic that works based on such simple ideas – one rhythmic pattern, one chord, one texture – last so much longer than conventional symphonies or sonatas. The timescales of minimalist or minimalist-based pieces are often massive, maximal: Philip Glass's *Music in 12 Parts* lasts about four hours, Steve Reich's *Drumming* for sixty minutes and more, Terry Riley's *In C* can last twenty minutes or an hour and a half, despite the fact that you could play all the musical material in these pieces in a shorter space of time than it takes to play one of Anton Webern's tiny, expressionist works.

But that's the point: to experience the changing of perception that this music is all about, you need to spend time with it. And that's my counter-intuitive advice to anyone who doesn't think they like this music: listen to more of it, for longer. That's especially true for music like La Monte Young's *Composition 1960 #7* – a single interval, a fifth – marked to be played 'for a long time'. That could mean minutes, months, or years.

For all their diversity, what connects all these works is a profound exploration of the fundamentals of music – opening up new kinds of experience as they experiment with new kinds of rhythms and silences, repetitions and drones. And along the way, giving us a new way of hearing: a way of listening to the deep processes of how music works. Minimalism? Maximal-ism, more like, in its impact on musical culture and the way it can change your listening life.

- ◀ Steve Reich: *Piano Phase*
- ◀ Dennis Johnson: *November*
- ◀ Éliane Radigue: *Trilogie de la mort*, no. 1, 'Kyema'
- ◀ Mike Oldfield: *Tubular Bells*
- ◀ Michael Nyman: 'Prawn Watching', from the soundtrack for *A Zed and Two Noughts*

58

Earworms

They're with us all the time: alien musical interlopers that stalk the darkest regions of our memories – unbidden, unwanted, uncontrollable – and start to play on an unending loop, without stopping, wheels within wheels, churning through our brains. Earworms!

The Germans have the best word for this psycho-musical phenomenon: *Ohrwürmer*, which literally translates as 'earworms', but is also the German word for 'earwigs' – appropriately, since the idea of these pieces of music as insectoid invaders of your brain matches the experience of living with Lady Gaga's 'Bad Romance' and 'La donna è mobile' from Giuseppe Verdi's *Rigoletto* hour after hour, day after day. Nobody chooses their earworms – we feel that they choose us, emerging into our subconscious as aural-hallucinatory zombies. So what turns a tune into a potential brain-invader? And can we do anything to stop them?

The musicologist Kelly Jakubowski has analysed what makes a tune more likely to turn into an earworm, and the three major factors are that they need to be 'not too simple and not too complex', have a largely predictable or symmetrical melodic contour, but also feature a memorable quirk, like an unexpected leap between notes. So it makes sense that Ronnie

Hazlehurst's theme tune for *Some Mothers Do 'Ave 'Em*, with its quirkily unforgettable tune for two piccolos, is jostling for earworm-supremacy in my brain with an unpredictably energetic tune from Rachmaninoff's *Symphonic Dances*: both are instantly memorable, yet piquantly surprising – and totally unlodgeable from my waking and sleeping hours.

Mark Twain took the idea of obsessive earworms to a logical and horrifying extreme in a story he wrote in 1876, originally called 'A Literary Nightmare'. The narrator of this tale is helplessly possessed by some 'jingling rhymes': 'My head kept humming . . . I drifted downtown, and presently discovered that my feet were keeping time to that relentless jingle.' Even asleep, he 'rolled, tossed, and jingled all night long'. The story gets worse, because in a nightmare anticipating *Invasion of the Body Snatchers*, he passes the tune on to his pastor, who impregnates the whole congregation with this devilish musical earwig. A whole community infected by the same earworm – the horror!

But maybe there is a way to get rid of them. Some scientists recommend listening through to the end of the song or piece that your particular earworm comes from, to exorcise its power by hearing it in context rather than on a never-ending loop. I'm happy to do that with Rachmaninoff's *Symphonic Dances*, but watching a whole series of *Some Mothers Do 'Ave 'Em* might be less appealing. Others say we've no choice but to give ourselves over to the torment of the *Ohrwürmer*, and know that when *Black Beauty* or *Indiana Jones* or Kylie Minogue ends, there will always be another to replace it.

And maybe that's no bad thing. Earworms are probably the music we hear most often in our lives, given that it's our minds that play these tunes for us. And whether we like it or not, they tell us more about our psychology than we might like to admit.

So don't try and stop them: let's celebrate our earworms, a sub-conscious selection as individual as we all are as human beings.

- ◀ Dexys Midnight Runners: 'Come On Eileen', from *Too-Rye-Ay*
- ◀ Kylie Minogue: 'Can't Get You Out of My Head', from *Fever*
- ◀ Giuseppe Verdi: 'La donna è mobile', from *Rigoletto*, Act 3
- ◀ Rihanna: 'Umbrella', from *Good Girl Gone Bad* (featuring Jay-Z)
- ◀ Kool & the Gang: 'Let's Go Dancing', from *As One*

59

Concertos: all for one and one for all?

Pity the loneliness of the long-distance concerto soloist: imagine the fear and trepidation they must feel before they go out there at the Royal Albert Hall, at Symphony Hall in Birmingham, or the Royal Concert Hall in Glasgow. We in the audience are cruel and epicurean voyeurs who come to listen and to judge: impress us or be damned. Another feat of memory ahead of them, another evening at the world's most exposing, terrifying and gladiatorial office. It's a drama that plays out, night after night, on the stages of concert halls all over the world.

They are all miracle-working musical superheroes, our soloists who dare to scale the heights of Mozart, Shosta-kovich, Musgrave, Xenakis and all the rest. So how did the concerto become a simultaneously glamorous and gladiator-ial combat between the individual and the collective – one against all? It wasn't always this way. The origins of the word 'concerto' aren't definitive, but it could be a fusion of Latin words that denote both a weaving together and a tussle. And in early eighteenth-century concertos – like those for string instruments by Arcangelo Corelli – the music is more a weaving together between a smaller group and a larger one than it is a competition, a collaboration rather than a duel.

That's true, too, in Antonio Vivaldi's hundreds of concertos and J. S. Bach's Brandenburgs, but when we get to the nineteenth and twentieth centuries, the discourse becomes much more about a spotlit soloist distinguished from the massed orchestral group behind them – from Beethoven's five piano concertos to Brahms's two, from Shostakovich's concertos for cello to John Adams's Violin Concerto.

The reason the form survives and thrives – as it continues to in new dimensions, forms and multi-media performances in twenty-first-century concertos – is because of the mixture of empathy and awe we feel as an audience when we watch soloists perform with and against an orchestra. We feel with them, we watch their emotions writ large on their faces, their bodies, the way they move with their instruments. Soloists embody the music while it lasts, and because our attention is focused on them, we feel with and for them in their ever-changing emotional relationship with the orchestral musicians.

We might not be able to do what they do, but like all those soloists up there, we are individuals too, who are shaped by our relationships with the collectives in our lives – our families, our societies, our colleagues, our cultures. Every concerto ever written, from Arcangelo Corelli to Philip Venables, is another chapter in the story of those possibilities between us and them, between ourselves and all the others in our lives. That's why we have not just a love, but also a human need for concertos in our musical lives. Gladiators and heroines, collaborators and empathisers: soloists of the world, we salute you!

◀ Antonio Vivaldi: *The Four Seasons*, 'Spring'
◀ Wolfgang Amadé Mozart: Concerto no. 5 for violin in A major, K219
◀ John Adams: Violin Concerto
◀ György Ligeti: Violin Concerto
◀ Philip Venables: *Venables plays Bartók* (violin concerto)

60

What's the point of practice?

'Practice makes perfect', as the saying goes. So why is musical practice so often a chore, whether we're child-like beginners or fully fledged pros, starter pianists or virtuosos of the world's stages?

There's a theory spearheaded by the writer Malcolm Gladwell that if you want to get good at anything – playing the violin, throwing the javelin, becoming a surgeon, turning yourself into a chess grandmaster – you need to have devoted at least ten thousand hours, around ten years of your learning life, to practising it. Gladwell isn't saying that you need no native talent at all, or that you can mindlessly spend ten thousand hours chucking yourself at javelins, or vainly throwing your fingers at the same Mozart sonata I've been trying to play for decades, and emerge by some miraculous osmosis at the other end of your ten-thousand-hour hell-tunnel of practice with the technical equipment and musical and physical prowess of a Fatima Whitbread or a Vladimir Horowitz. But he is saying you need the graft as much as you need the talent. So get grafting!

The problem is – it doesn't work, as research from Princeton University has proven. Instead of ten thousand hours, Princeton's research says you need an unpredictable alchemy of talent, application, supportive circumstances and sheer luck.

Which is why music history is littered with the career-corpses of those who didn't quite make it, whose practice didn't make perfect. Robert Schumann was one of them: he knew that as a pianist he wasn't in the same league as his wife Clara, one of the nineteenth century's most famous virtuosos. Robert had a problem with the flexibility of his fingers, and the relative paralysis of the second and third fingers of his right hand. It's likely this condition was brought on by treatment for Robert's syphilis – inhalation of mercury fumes, or mercury poisoning we would now call it – but he was determined to find a way through his affliction. That meant abiding by the medical strictures of the day, including 'putting the affected part into the thoracic or abdominal cavity of a freshly slaughtered animal and keeping it there as long as the natural warmth lasted' – this was genuine medical advice that both he and Clara observed throughout their lives. And as well as powders and bandages and freshly slaughtered thoraxes, Robert used some kind of mechanical device to improve his fingers' dexterity. None of it worked.

On one hand, there are no short cuts – but on the other, if you ain't got it, you just ain't got it. Even more fundamentally, there is no such thing as the 'perfect' that is the goal of practice, according to the saying. And once you accept that you can't ever reach that Parnassus of perfection, whether you're among virtuosos like Nicola Benedetti or Stephen Hough or James Rhodes – all of whom have spoken publicly about the pressures of practice – or whether you're starting out on your musical journey, the idea of practising becomes much more pleasurable. Stephen Hough says that when he makes his first mistake in a performance, he's suddenly more relaxed, because the pressure of perfection no longer hangs over him. Released from that terrible and vacuous genie, he can concentrate on what music-making is really about: the communication of human emotion and experience from one body to another.

So practice doesn't make perfect, and thank goodness for that. We're all gloriously imperfect – which is exactly as it should be. Be yourself: don't practise, just play. Or as Yoda puts it in *Star Wars*, 'Do or do not. There is no try.'

◀ Frédéric Chopin: *Études*
◀ Béla Bartók: *Mikrokosmos*
◀ Carl Czerny: *One Hundred Progressive Studies*, op. 139
◀ Wolfgang Amadé Mozart: Piano Concerto no. 27 in B flat major, K595, first movement
◀ Charles-Louis Hanon: *The Virtuoso Pianist in Sixty Exercises*

61

Are we going to run out of tunes?

I noticed something recently. I was leaning on a lamp-post the other day and a George Formby-shaped earworm popped into my brain. I realised that Formby must have been a super-keen Wagnerian, because the first four notes of 'Leaning on a Lamp-post' are the same notes, in the same order – with admittedly different orchestration and philosophical overtones – as those from the Grail music in the outer acts of Richard Wagner's 'stage-festival consecration play', *Parsifal*. Of course: the search for the healing of Amfortas's psycho-sexual wound, and the Godot-like waiting for Formby's life-partner who never arrives. Coincidence? I think not!

The thing is, once you start noticing these melodic connections, there's an endless well of similarities out there in the world of tunes, across genres, times, and places. John Williams knew his Richard Strauss well enough to realise he was consciously paraphrasing Strauss's tone-poem *Death and Transfiguration* in the love theme of his music for the movie *Superman*. Queen needed to steal from Leoncavallo in their 'It's a Hard Life'; Procol Harum plundered from Bach in 'A Whiter Shade of Pale'. Mika nicked Rossini's 'Largo al factotum' in his song 'Grace Kelly', while Frank Sinatra's 'Full Moon and Empty Arms' comes from Rachmaninoff's Second Piano Concerto.

Just as Mozart steals from Handel's *Messiah* in his Requiem, Schubert quotes Beethoven's Ninth in his 'Great' C major symphony, and the White Stripes pilfer from Anton Bruckner's Fifth Symphony in their song 'Seven Nation Army'.

Don't these borrowings and coincidences – as well as the dozens of court cases about musical origination in recent years, from Led Zeppelin to Ed Sheeran – prove that we're running out of tunes? Not according to the mathematician and geometer of musical space Marcus du Sautoy, who says there's no need to worry, because the number of tunes available even within the limitations of the twelve notes of the Western scale is greater than the number of human beings who will ever live.

I know that Marcus du Sautoy is mathematically right, but why are there so many similarities in the way our tunes are made? It's as if there's a series of Venn diagrams that connects them together, so that Queen becomes Leoncavallo becomes Wagner becomes George Formby, all swimming together in the not-quite-infinite melodic ocean of statistical possibility.

What's remarkable about the way all these melodies work is that though they can be so similar to one another, we remember them as separate, distinct musical life-forms. It's not that they're all original: it's as if they have the same individuality yet the same connection to each other as we all do as human beings. We are all made from the same stuff of mostly water and carbon, and most of us share a similar arrangement of limbs and organs, and a roughly similar collection of facial features. And yet we're all different. And just as the whole human comedy goes on renewing itself, the same goes for the almost endless biology of tunes. They too are made of distinct arrangements of the same musical stuff of notes and rhythms. Yet they're never going to run out on us, even as they refer to each other and relate to each other. The never-ending carousel of melodic connection just keeps on perpetuating itself.

- ◀ George Formby: 'I'm Leaning on a Lamp-post' (Noel Gay)
- ◀ Richard Wagner: *Parsifal*, Act 1, 'Grail Scene'
- ◀ Beyoncé: 'Single Ladies (Put A Ring On It)', from *I Am . . . Sasha Fierce*
- ◀ Mark-Anthony Turnage: *Hammered Out*
- ◀ Frank Sinatra: 'Full Moon and Empty Arms' (Buddy Kaye and Ted Mossman)

62

Codes, ciphers, enigmas

Music in code: whether it's Bach or Schumann, Berg or Shostakovich translating their names, their lovers, their superstitions and their spiritual lives into musical notation, or Pink Floyd recording messages into their middle-eights that you can only hear when you play the record backwards, musicians have relished an almost occult facility for encoding messages into the notes they write, play and record.

But in the litany of musical codes that still need to be cracked, one piece looms above all others, composed by a brilliant amateur cryptologist who said that his music concealed a secret that he would take to his grave – and he did: Edward Elgar's 'Enigma' Variations. The mystery stems from a comment that Elgar made in a programme note, claiming that the theme we hear at the start of the piece, the basis for the variations, isn't the actual 'Enigma' tune. Instead the true theme is an unheard melody that can be played simultaneously with what the orchestra plays at the opening. But for over a century, no one has been able to identify that mystery melody once and for all. According to Elgar, 'It is so well known that it is extraordinary that no one has spotted it.' But he also said that the theme we actually hear conceals a 'dark saying [that] must be left unguessed . . . The enigma I will not explain' – and he was true to his word until his death in 1934.

Many solutions have been suggested by musicological sleuthers, from 'Auld Lang Syne' to the second movement of Mozart's 'Prague' Symphony, from Liszt's *Les Préludes* to 'Rule, Britannia!', or the hymns 'Ein feste Burg' and 'Now the Day is Over'. Yet none of them can be proved as the definitive solution. The numerals of pi have also been suggested – and why? Because when you translate the first four numbers of pi – 3.142 – into the steps of a minor scale, you get the first four notes of the tune we hear at the start of the 'Enigma' Variations. We know that Elgar loved numerical cryptograms, and the Indiana Pi Bill had been passed in 1897 (just before he started work on the piece), which attempted to legislate the value of the infinite fractions of pi: QED, pi is the answer.

Or maybe not. All of these supposed 'solutions' to the enigma of the 'Enigma' only take us further away from the piece. The real riddle of this music lies in the compositional brilliance that creates something that means so many different things to all of us. We want to search for a single solution to explain the impact of a piece of music that means so much, that conjures such an instant melancholic ache, as in the 'Nimrod' variation, or that carries us on a wave of irresistible excitement, as in the final movement, 'E. D. U.', Elgar's musical self-portrait. We feel this music's mysterious power, and we want there to be a single explanation for it.

But as the story of the endless 'Enigma'-sleuthing proves, just when you think you've got the answer, it slips through our grasp. What's left is the experience of the music, which doesn't stand for anything apart from itself, which we can yet interpret in infinite ways. Elgar's enigma is really the ultimate riddle of all the most powerful music – a puzzle we can never truly solve.

- ◀ Robert Schumann: *Fantasie* in C major, op. 17
- ◀ Dmitri Shostakovich: Symphony no. 10 in E minor, finale
- ◀ Pink Floyd: 'Empty Spaces', from *The Wall*
- ◀ The Royal Doulton Band: 'Now the Day is Over'
- ◀ Edward Elgar: Variations on an Original Theme, 'Enigma'

63

Interpretation – more than the score

Radio 3 listener Eleanor Ironside summed up the question of interpretation – all those different performances and recordings of the same pieces that make up the culture of classical music – like this:

> When I went to buy my first ever classical album (I was young) I asked in the serious classical shop for a recording of *The Young Person's Guide to the Orchestra*. The man serving me asked which recording of it was I looking for, to which I replied: 'What difference does it make?' To which he replied: 'What difference does it make?!?' To this day I have never discovered the answer to that question, because I haven't dared ask it again.

Well, Eleanor: an answer there must be, because it's one of the most fundamental features of the cultures of classical music. I remember versions of exactly the same conversation, but from another perspective: when I was a teenager, trying to defend the fact to bemused friends that I was saving up to buy different performances by three conductors of exactly the same piece, Mozart's 'Jupiter' Symphony; Karl Böhm's luxurious grandiloquence as well as the energised momentum of

Charles Mackerras and the cosmos-bothering complexity of Nikolaus Harnoncourt.

Three recordings that may as well have been three different pieces, for the distinctive emotional experiences they unleashed. And if all that's true within just three of the hundreds of recordings and thousands of different performances there have ever been of Mozart's Symphony no. 41 in C major, since it was new in 1788, how on earth can we say that there is a single concept contained within the phrase 'Mozart's "Jupiter" Symphony'? How can there possibly be a definitive version or recording of such a sprawlingly amorphous concept as this Mozart symphony, or any other piece of classical music?

Think about the stretchy boundaries of the thing we call 'Beethoven's Fifth Symphony', which belongs to Carlos Kleiber conducting the Vienna Philharmonic, and to Walter Murphy in his funked-up version of the piece in 'A Fifth of Beethoven', and to the Portsmouth Sinfonia, who produce a passionate cacophony in which amateurs – and professionals playing instruments that aren't their own – attempt to play the notes in front of them. Walter Murphy's and the Portsmouth Sinfonia's versions of Beethoven seem to belong to a different class of performance to Kleiber and the Vienna Phil, but they're really only a question of degree: if you can change the speed you play the notes, and the size of the orchestra, if you can interpret all those parameters, as Kleiber does, it's only a question of allowing the same freedom to turn it into a disco anthem, like Walter Murphy, or to gloriously yet honestly distort it, as the Portsmouth Sinfonia do – they're still Beethoven's Fifth. As Beethoven himself said: 'To play a wrong note is insignificant; to play without passion is inexcusable!'

Back to Eleanor's question: what difference does it make, between performances, between recordings? All those differences are the true substance of classical music as an art-form: essential, life-enhancing differences that are sounded in every concert we experience, and every new recording we hear.

So instead of trying to find solutions to all those differences, forget about finding the best recording, or the one performance to rule them all, and let's jump into the life-giving sea of endless interpretation that this music will always inspire.

◀ Ludwig van Beethoven: Symphony no. 5 in C minor, op. 67 (Carlos Kleiber, Vienna Philharmonic Orchestra)
◀ Ludwig van Beethoven: Symphony no. 5 in C minor, op. 67 (Portsmouth Sinfonia)
◀ Walter Murphy: 'A Fifth of Beethoven'
◀ Anton Bruckner: Symphony no. 7 in E major (Sergiu Celibidache, Munich Philharmonic Orchestra)
◀ Anton Bruckner: Symphony no. 7 in E major (Roger Norrington, Stuttgart Radio Symphony Orchestra)

64

Pranked! Musical hoaxes

What connects the following together: six lost-then-found piano sonatas by Joseph Haydn; Tomaso Albinoni's *Adagio*; Piotr Zak's *Mobile for Tape and Percussion*, Louis Couperin's *La Précieuse*, the entire career of the Danish composer Dag Henrik Esrum-Hellerup, and the genre of the Funerary Violin?

The answer is: they are all musical fakes, hoaxes, forgeries, and inventions made by scurrilous and brilliant musicians and scholars to confound, satirise and delight. Albinoni's supposedly eighteenth-century *Adagio* is really the work of the twentieth-century musicologist Remo Giazotto; the violinist Fritz Kreisler composed that 'Couperin' piece; Hans Keller and Susan Bradshaw invented Zak's music; and Rohan Kriwaczek wrote an astoundingly rich history of the Funerary Violin that never actually happened.

But the strange and wonderful value of musical hoaxes – whether they're benignly comic in their intention, like Robert Layton's invention of Esrum-Hellerup in *The New Grove Dictionary of Music and Musicians* (1980 edition), or genuinely duplicitous, like Winfried Michel's brilliantly successful duping of the world with the six sonatas he passed off as Haydn's – is what they tell us about how we conceive of the value of musical works. For classical music culture it turns out that who wrote it is often more important than what it actually sounds like.

The Haydn story is a classic of the hoaxing genre. The leading Haydn scholar, H. C. Robbins Landon, said that these pieces 'clarify in a peculiarly striking way Haydn's search for a new musical language of strength and beauty which was to emerge as the beginning of the Viennese Classical Style; for many, the culmination of music in the Western world'. That was his reaction in the January 1994 edition of the *BBC Music Magazine*. The next month, he had to retract his belief in the authenticity of Haydn's sonatas. 'It now appears that the six Haydn sonatas are indeed likely to be a rather sinister forgery.' At least Robbins Landon never lost faith in the quality of the music: 'If they are forgeries they are master forgeries. In fact the work of the greatest forger of all time.'

But it turns out that musical quality isn't enough to guarantee music a place in the canons of classical music. The fact that it's now been comprehensively shown that these pieces really are fakes means that these six sonatas are lost again, because pianists don't play them, concert halls don't programme them, and they have been completely discarded by music history.

Which makes no sense at all: if these sonatas are good enough to have been thought to be by Haydn, why does their value suddenly disappear when we know they're by somebody else? Is the worth of a piece of music determined only by who wrote it, rather than what it actually is, what it sounds like? For so much classical culture, the answer is – yes.

But I think instead we need to have faith in fakes, like Michel's, like Kreisler's and Kriwaczek's. Because if we can't hear the musical value of these creative concoctions, we can't distinguish musical value in music that's supposedly authentic

– whatever that means. There is such a thing as fake news, but there can't be such a thing as fake music: whoever wrote it, or whoever we think wrote it, there is a real piece and a real repertoire there. Just like those piano sonatas, by Haydn, or not by Haydn – who cares? Enjoy the music!

- ◀ Rohan Kriwaczek ('Hieronymous Gratchenfleiss'): 'The Sombre Coquetry of Death', from *The Art of Funerary Violin*
- ◀ Fritz Kreisler ('Louis Couperin'): 'La Précieuse'
- ◀ Winfried Michel ('Joseph Haydn'): Sonata no. 23 in B minor
- ◀ Hans Keller and Susan Bradshaw ('Piotr Zak'): *Mobile* for Tape and Percussion
- ◀ Remo Giazotto ('Tomaso Albinoni'): *Adagio* in G minor

65

Parapapampam: Christmas music

Christmas – Kitschmas more like: what is it about Christmas that means we indulge in the tasteless rapture of music that's the aural equivalent of figgy pudding and mistletoe, Coke-sponsored Santa Clauses, and glittery baby Jesuses? From Michael Ball to Charlotte Church's back catalogue, Michael Bublé to Katherine Jenkins, from *Karajan: The Christmas Album* to Elisabeth Schwarzkopf's festive compilation, from Noddy Holder to John Rutter: at Christmas we lose ourselves in musical cheese as at no other time of the year.

And diving into that Yuletide fondue, there's that word, 'kitsch': it conjures up a definite set of feelings, images and products. Kitsch is that Christmas-card image of a cottage in a forest, with festive cheer glowing through the windows, groaning under a few feet of Disney-perfect snow: it's something artificial, over-the-top, and above all, for sale. Yet for something so clearly understood, the origins of the word are lost in the mists of nostalgic time. 'Kitsch' probably comes from Munich's Christmas markets in the 1860s and 1870s, when it was coined by marketeers selling their souvenirs; or it may be derived from words that mean to cheapen or to smear; or it might be a corruption of the French 'chic'.

And when it's turned into musical and commercial gold, the

187

genius of the kitschified nostalgia of, say, Bing Crosby's performance of Irving Berlin's 'White Christmas' is that it expresses a yearning for a time that never actually existed. Those Christmases Bing says he 'used to know' are a candy-cane concoction that have only ever been true in the minds of Christmas-card artists and Hollywood producers. Bing's intimate delivery from underneath a sonic snowdrift of celeste, close-harmony choir and swooping strings is a sound of gorgeously irresistible nostalgia, the sound of false Christmas consciousness and fake memories for times we never shared with Bing, or with anyone else.

So kitsch is superficial, sentimental, manipulative, commercial, beneath consideration of all who consider themselves of sound taste and good mind and . . . what snobbish rot! I love it. And admit it: you do too.

The axiom of the festive season is that there is an irresistible urge to put feeling before rationality, and for once in the year, to be taken on a tide of love for this music, whether it's the kitschification of classical, heavy metal or hip-hop. Let critical judgements be left aside for another day: there are no such things as guilty pleasures at Christmas – there is only pleasure.

And that's the great truth that Christmas music can teach us. The world glows with the generosity of its pleasures during the festive season, opening up emotions that may be exquisitely manufactured and manipulated, but which are no less real for that – across the world, across genres, across the infinite aeons of nostalgia. Happy Kitschmas!

- Chris Rea: 'Driving Home for Christmas', from *On the Beach*
- Irving Berlin: 'White Christmas' (Bing Crosby)
- James Lord Pierpont: 'Jingle Hell' (Christopher Lee)
- John Rutter: 'Star Carol'
- Helmut Lachenmann: *The Little Match Girl*

66

How to love new music

On our travels through the musical universe, there's one kind of music that seems to have a harder time than most in making the leap into the hearts of listeners. It's music that goes under the banner of the contemporary, the dissonant, the discordant: the sort of thing that critics have called a 'blood-curdling nightmare', 'the cacophony of the present', or an 'odious meowing . . . [with] discords enough to split the hardiest ear'.

But, those descriptions probably weren't about the music you thought they were. In fact, those critical reactions were inspired by Beethoven's Fifth Symphony – that was the 'odious meowing', according to the Russian writer and critic Alexander Oulibicheff; Liszt's *Faust Symphony* – a 'cacophonous racket', as heard by the *New York Musical Review*; and Richard Strauss's tone-poem *Till Eulenspiegel* – enough to curdle the blood, according to the *Boston Herald*.

That's the point about music throughout history: it was all new, once, and those kind of reactions reveal what Nicholas Slonimsky in his brilliant *Lexicon of Musical Invective* called the 'non-acceptance of the unfamiliar', which has affected and afflicted music since records began.

So if you think you've got a problem with today's contemporary music, that's a mere historical illusion. Take a piece like

Harrison Birtwistle's *Earth Dances*, an elementally shattering orchestral piece made in 1986: dissonant, unpredictable, violent and wild in its contrasts of orchestral strata – music that's hard to listen to, surely?

Not at all: *Earth Dances* is easier to feel, to understand, to be awed by, than music by, say, Mozart or Haydn. And why? Because it's not designed to make an impact based on your knowledge of the conventions of classical harmony and form, and your appreciation of how the composer is manipulating our expectations within that style and structure. Instead, Birtwistle's *Earth Dances* has an instantly geological impact: it's like being on the edge of a sea cliff or a mountain ridge. When you listen to *Earth Dances*, you're consumed by it. The question isn't whether you love it or not, but the intensity that your body and brain experience. When Birtwistle reaches into the guts of the lowest sounds an orchestra can make, you feel you're part of a process of musical creation that returns to the gigantic violence that forged every element we breathe or see or touch: inside the crucibles of supernova explosions, or folded into the strata of the rocks beneath your feet.

That's just one example of how supposedly dissonant music is easier to appreciate than music of eighteenth- or nineteenth-century refinement. There are many more. The London Sinfonietta once ran an education project for schools using the music of Maurice Ravel and Edgard Varèse. One of the composers was instantly appealing to the children, while the other was too remote and too difficult. No surprise, since one of these composers wrote music with 'no mercy in its disharmony . . . successions of screaming, clashing, plangorous discords' according to *Musical America*. Yet that was the music the children connected with the most: they loved Varèse's violently impactful sounds, whereas

Ravel's more conventional sensuality was austerely difficult to relate to.

You want an immediately visceral musical experience? Listen to Birtwistle, Xenakis, Lachenmann, Lutyens, Saariaho or Varèse; ground-breaking music that will sear your imagination and plunge you into a world of irresistible, elemental feeling. And while you're at it, remember that all music is new music – it's only a question of historical perspective. And unlike those critics, accept the unfamiliar!

◀ Richard Strauss: *Till Eulenspiegels lustige Streiche*
◀ Harrison Birtwistle: *Earth Dances*
◀ Iannis Xenakis: *Keqrops* for piano and orchestra
◀ Elisabeth Lutyens: music for the film *The Skull*
◀ Stormzy: 'Own It', from *Heavy is the Head* (featuring Ed Sheeran and Burna Boy)

67

Why are classical audiences so quiet?

What are we allowed to do as listeners in concert halls and opera houses? There are really just two things that classical music culture sanctions as available behaviours: we are supposed to be quiet, and applaud – but only in the right places. Yet it never used to be like this. It's a profound irony that when the vast majority of music that's now played in concert halls and opera houses was actually composed, it was written for a different kind of audience – a much noisier, much more participative one.

Symphonies and string quartets and operas weren't supposed to be approached in the same way we attend a library, or a funeral – in reverence and deference; instead, these pieces of music, from Monteverdi's operas in the seventeenth century to Elgar's symphonies in the twentieth, were designed for our involvement. Silence was just one of the options available to us: we would encore movements, clapping so vehemently after the scherzo or the slow movement that the performers would just have to play it again; we would exclaim, holler, and comment on the performance as it was going on.

That picture of participative listening is so unfamiliar today that you might think I've lost the audience-applauding plot. But I have evidence: in 1778, the twenty-two-year-old

Mozart made his debut at the Concert Spirituel in Paris, and he wrote a D major symphony especially tailored to the listening culture and expectations of the city. Here's what happened, in his own words, in the final movement:

> Having observed that all last as well as first allegros
> here begin together with all the other instruments, and
> generally unisono, mine commenced with only two violins,
> piano for the first eight bars, followed instantly by a forte;
> the audience, as I expected, called out 'Shh!!!' at the soft
> beginning, and the instant the forte was heard began to
> clap their hands.

That's first-hand evidence about a piece of music composed for the audience's fully engaged, fully noisy participation. And not only between the movements, but within them: this is music that's actually composed around what Mozart knew would be the noisy appreciation of that audience. If that noise hadn't happened during the concert, this piece would have been judged by Mozart as a failure.

Haydn's symphonies – the most popular orchestral music in Paris and the rest of Europe at the time – are full of these kind of games of give-and-take with our listening, and we know that Beethoven's symphonies were received in the early nineteenth century in the same way, with applause, encoring, noisy participation, approval and criticism.

So what changed? Stendhal, Rossini's biographer, identified a worrying trend at the opera in Paris by 1824: people started being quiet. 'What will result from this scrupulous silence and continuous attention? That fewer people will enjoy themselves.' I think Stendhal has been proved right: the listening cultures of classical music have only become more quiet and more censorious to our bodies and their noises over the centuries since his comment.

Our listening needs to be noisier today – in order to be more respectful to our place in musical culture. For Mozart's symphonies and Rossini's operas and Tchaikovsky's concertos to be fully realised as musical events, we need to be much more than passive listening freight carted in and out of concert halls. To make these pieces of music come alive, and even to save the thing called 'classical music' – we need to make some noise.

◀ Wolfgang Amadé Mozart: Symphony no. 31 in D major, K297, 'Paris'
◀ Gustav Mahler: Symphony no. 5, fourth movement
◀ Jean-Philippe Rameau: *Platée*
◀ Antonio Vivaldi: *The Four Seasons*, 'Spring'
◀ Piotr Ilyich Tchaikovsky: Piano Concerto no. 1 in B flat minor, first movement

68

Orientalism and the music of elsewhere

What's the point at which our image of other cultures becomes a stereotypical cliché? And if we're using musical influences of other cultures, what are we really doing as a culture of composers, performers and listeners? Are we integrating the musical inspirations of Africa, China, Japan, Indonesia into our musical languages, or creating new hybrids from them? Or are we simply stealing from them, transplanting their music into new contexts in ways that radically alter their original contexts?

What we're talking about is orientalism: the term coined by Edward Said in his hugely influential book of that name, which set out the idea that a culture defines itself in relation to its others, to the things that it isn't. The orientalist gaze works one way: orientalism is what the West does to the East, making images and sounds of the Orient that are caricatures; appropriating, fantasising, othering. You can hear that process in whole repertoires of classical music, from Mozart's impression of Turkish music in the *Rondo alla Turca* from his A major piano sonata, to Beethoven's Janissary band at the end of his Ninth Symphony; or, most spectacularly, in Rimsky-Korsakov's pseudo-Arabian embodiment in *Scheherazade* of the exotic others of femininity, polyamory, and the worst excesses of the jaded bloodlust of a sexually voracious monarch.

And yet the Hungarian composer György Ligeti shows in his piano *Études* what can happen when a musician attends deeply to the music of other cultures: Ligeti creates a two-way conversation between the repertoires of the Ennanga harp music and the Amadinda xylophone music of Uganda, which inspired him, and his own cultural horizons. In Wolfgang Burde's study of his music, Ligeti himself says that the thrill of the first etude, 'Désordre' ('Disorder'), comes from 'pulsations of eight eighth notes [quavers] . . . already here we find the influence of Africa, 3+5 pulses, and this kind of asymmetry is also found in Latin American commercial folklore, in the Brazilian samba, and in the Cuban rumba . . . we find a combination of African thought processes with European barlines'. The connection between African traditions and Ligeti's compositions isn't to do with superficial 'Africanisms' or what the American composer Steve Reich calls the 'old exoticism trip'. As the musicologist Martin Scherzinger has written, Ligeti's *Études* open 'up new ways of hearing African music no less than Western music: the former as abstract art and the latter as embodied practice'. That's a two-way exchange – not just of musical ideas, but of ways of listening.

The Korean composer Unsuk Chin was a pupil of Ligeti's at the same time he was writing his *Études*. And Chin's music is similarly open to influences from South-East Asian musical traditions like gamelan, and yet committed to finding its own language in the traditions of modernist music: *Šu*, Chin's concerto for sheng and orchestra, is just one example of the way her deep hearing of both Western modernism and South-East Asian traditional music expand her creative possibilities – and the imagination of all of us listening.

What's the difference between orientalist fantasy and deeply considered creative use of musical material? It's in the ears of the composers, of course – but it's in our power, too, as listeners. In Japan, the tune we know as 'Auld Lang Syne' is called 'Hotaru no Hikari', 'Light of Fireflies', after the Meiji dynasty took tunes from the West to symbolise a new cultural openness. It's now a Japanese tune as much as it's a British or Scottish one. Orientalism? Exoticism? It just depends on where you're listening from, and how you're listening.

- ◀ 'Hotaru no Hikari' ('Light of Fireflies')
- ◀ Unsuk Chin: *Šu*, for sheng and orchestra
- ◀ György Ligeti: 'Désordre', *Étude* no. 1 for solo piano
- ◀ Ssaza Chief Kago and Danieri Seruwaniko: 'Oyagala Nkole Ntya'
- ◀ Claude Debussy: 'Pagodes' from *Estampes*

69

Can music be gendered?

When we're talking about music, we don't have a single equivalent word for the 'gaze' in the visual arts. And yet it's there: and the point about the auditory 'gaze', or 'way of hearing', is that it's never neutral. For much writing in the fields of both music history and cultural politics, that way of hearing has been constructed as male: a masculine 'gaze' has dominated the discourse.

Take the music of Ethel Smyth: her operas such as *The Wreckers*, *The Boatswain's Mate* and *Fête Galante*, or her orchestral music and sacred works. If you know Smyth's distinctively late-Romantic style – its drama and clarity, its expressive power and lyrical persuasion – you know that her music belongs alongside the other composers of her generation, like Richard Strauss, or Edward Elgar, as a vital part of our collective musical history.

But in her lifetime, the kinds of reaction Smyth faced from her fellow musicians and critics were patronising and misogynistic. In 1892, after a performance of her *Overture to Antony and Cleopatra*, George Bernard Shaw wrote in *The World*, 'When E. M. Smyth's heroically brassy overture . . . was finished, and the composer called to the platform, it was observed with stupefaction that all that tremendous noise had been made by a lady.' Shaw illuminates not only his own prejudices, but the audience's, who had their gendered expectations overturned so completely by Smyth's 'heroic' and 'noisy' music: a woman came up with that! Who would have thunk it?

Shaw was writing in a critical tradition in which instrumental music – with no words, and no obvious subject – was nonetheless framed by gender politics. The first music theorist to formalise this way of thinking was A. B. Marx: in 1845, Marx's music theory talked about the contrast between the two main themes in pieces in sonata form (the dominant structure in nineteenth-century instrumental music) in terms of a difference between a 'masculine' first theme, with its 'primary freshness and energy . . . energetically, emphatically, absolutely shaped', and a feminine second subject, 'milder, more supple'. Marx shows that supposedly abstract musical form was often understood as nothing of the kind, but as a kind of musical Adam and Eve story in which Adam was in charge.

So let's wrench forward to the present day: what if you were to compose a piece that was about turning that male way of hearing and composing inside-out, so that a piece wasn't about masculinity, but femininity? That's what generations of composers like Laura Bowler are doing right now: Bowler's /fɛmɪˈnɪnɪti/ is a vividly essential multi-media rage against mechanised stereotypes of femininity – in culture in general, and in musical culture in particular.

And yet music, of all the arts, offers the greatest opportunity for experiences that can perform multiple identities, all at the same time. The final trio of Richard Strauss's 1911 opera, *Der Rosenkavalier*, features three female voices singing the roles of two women and a teenage boy: the Marschallin, a soprano, regrets that she is now middle-aged; her former lover, the teenage Octavian – sung by a mezzo-soprano who is always, obviously, a woman in the way Strauss writes for her – is in love with Sophie, another soprano. Strauss's music liquefies the categories of male or female, the lover and the beloved, the voyeur and the singer. The music's overwhelming lyricism gives us an experience which is simultaneously about the sexes – and exists between them. Strauss's trio is the sound of this fluidity, of transcended sex or gender – being the other as well as being with the other – of all true intimacy.

It's up to us to understand this in the way we hear music: to know that because there's no such thing as a pure music, we always have a choice about how we're listening. Music isn't the sound of our prejudices being reflected back to us – crudely conceived maleness or femaleness, or systems of power or politics that amplify our complacency. Music is also the sound of the other, and gives us an embodied experience that melts our preconceptions away, that shifts our boundaries, that dissolves our differences. Here's to the human ear.

◀ Alice Mary Smith: Symphony in A minor
◀ Ethel Smyth: Mass in D
◀ Laura Bowler: /ˈfɛmɪ ˈnɪnɪti/
◀ Grażyna Bacewicz: Concerto no. 1 for violin and orchestra
◀ Richard Strauss: 'Hab' mir's gelobt, ihn lieb zu haben', from *Der Rosenkavalier*, Act 3

70

What if . . . ? The marvellous musical multiverse

What if musical history had been different? What if we could travel to those multiverses that quantum physics says really should exist, a new one for each potential outcome to every decision we make, from which muesli to have for breakfast to which key our next symphony should be in? It's a place in which infinite doors stretch out from infinite corridors. All we have to do is open any door to find a new dimension: to those universes in which McCartney never met Lennon; Rodgers didn't know Hammerstein; Gilbert teamed up with Stevenson, not Sullivan; in which Alma Mahler kept composing and left Gustav in her wake; in which Buddy Holly lived to a hundred; and Jimi Hendrix is still doing stadium tours.

And if we type the dimensional co-ordinates into the *Listening Service* Universe Collider to reach Vienna, 5 December 1791, what might we find in an alternative universe? A thirty-five-year-old composer – Wolfie, as he's known – is under the weather, but he's fit enough to get through it. It's all part of life at a time when a glass of dirty water or a single mistimed sneeze could put you at the mercy of epidemiological chance. He's better by Christmas – just as well, he has a family to support – and he's recently landed a cushy job at court, writing sets of dances he churns out on a wet Tuesday afternoon, giving him time to compose the music he's really interested in: that's to say, a new repertoire of sacred music, a genre he's never quite cracked – until now.

Our composer is Mozart, and he doesn't die at thirty-five as he does in our universe: here, he lives till he's eighty. And in this particular universe, the Requiem that Mozart writes and completes in December 1791 is the start of a whole series of sacred pieces he composes throughout the 1810s and 1820s, in which he finds a new kind of crystalline classicism. He infused the fugues and Passions and oratorios of his favourite composer, Handel, with his own sacred storytelling, using everything he'd learnt in the secular forms of operas and symphonies to compose distilled but emotionally fearless Mass settings. In fact, the shape of this whole nineteenth century in music looks very different to ours: Mozart overshadows the grotesque crudity of that growling maverick, Beethoven, and the weird experiments in repetition and stasis of Franz Schubert.

And so many other journeys are possible through the multiverse of the musical what-ifs: what if Fanny Mendelssohn had been supported as a composer in the same way as her brother, Felix? What if Louise Farrenc had been promoted, published and feted in France? If Alma Mahler hadn't had to give up her composing ambitions when her husband Gustav forced her to choose between composing and marrying him? And if Pauline Viardot had felt as empowered as a composer as she did as a singer and teacher?

Our speculative journeys prove to me that the multiverses are real – even in our single universe. They're swirling around us all the time, because we're continually making choices, not only about what happens next in our lives, but about what happened in the past too – in our musical memories, and in the way we tell our musical histories.

Which means that the corridors of the infinitely conditional explode into our single universe: making it not a place of inevitability, but a field of possibility in which anything can happen – and everything probably has. Where next? What if there were a world in which you could hear Mozart on a hybrid instrument, part fortepiano, part harpsichord, a sort of musical pushmi-pullyu; or in which Beethoven composed for the Panharmonicon and cannon fire; and Chopin played the giraffe piano? Hold on – that's us, isn't it? Alternative realities, other musical universes – they're right here. Just keep asking the question – what if?

◀ Alma Mahler: 'In meines Vaters Garten'
◀ Robert Schumann: *Scenes from Goethe's 'Faust'*, scene 7
◀ Clara Schumann: Piano Concerto in A minor, third movement
◀ Louise Farrenc: Sextet in C minor for piano and winds, third movement
◀ Scott Joplin: 'A Real Slow Drag', from *Treemonisha*

71

Extreme classical!

Extremes! How do some pieces of music push the boundaries of what's possible, into the realms of the superhuman, not to say the cosmically absurd – in intention, and in performance? The whole of music history can be written as a story of extremes that are shocking at first, then heard as merely titillating, before being copied and accepted, after which what were originally innovations now become heard as conventional and 'classical' – whether that's the symphonic density of Mozart's 'Jupiter' Symphony, the scale of Beethoven's 'Eroica', or the rhythmic adventure of Stravinsky's ballet *The Rite of Spring*.

But there are also pieces that are, simply, out there: that can't be constrained by any musical convention, that can't be experienced in any single human lifespan, extremes of expression and idea that stretch our imaginations to breaking point. How about a performance of a piece that will take 639 years? John Cage's *Organ²/ASLSP (As Slow as Possible)* is under way at a church in Halberstadt in Germany. It started in 2001 – although the first note wasn't heard until seventeen months later, since the piece starts with a pause – and it won't finish until 2640, by which time advances in genetic science will no doubt mean we are all there to witness this piece's cosmic dissolution as the organ at last winds down.

The British composer Jem Finer has out-Caged Cage with his *Longplayer*: a piece that will play without repetition until 31 December 2999, having started on the stroke of the new millennium in locations all over the world. It's based on a piece that originally lasted just twenty minutes and twenty seconds, but its material is algorithmically processed so that nothing will repeat for one thousand years.

Mind not sufficiently boggled? Try this: the American band Bull of Heaven have dared to dream on a much, much bigger scale than either Cage or Finer. They have a series of pieces based on series of prime numbers, working out in sequences of sounds which coincide at ever greater lengths of time apart, like *287: n* – which lasts for eighty-seven trillion hours. But their longest ever piece is the magnificently dauntingly titled *310: ΩΣPx0(2^18×5^18)p*k*k*k*, which lasts for 3.343 quindecillion years. That's a number that starts with 3,343 and has forty-five zeros after it: a long, LONG time.

In 2014, Bull of Heaven's Clayton Counts talked to *Vice* magazine.

I . . . believe that absurdity is necessary in this world, especially in the arts. Music must confront . . . The time aspect . . . stems from our interest in mathematics and astronomy. We realised how small and insignificant we are. Man is only an unpredictable small particle in an ocean of repetitions. We try to match that ocean with those long pieces.

Confronting the cosmos: that's something that music and musicians have always used their extremities of imagination to do. Bull of Heaven's is a genuine music of the spheres, out there in the ocean of vast time.

- John Cage: *Organ²/ASLSP (As Slow as Possible)*
- Alexander Scriabin/Alexander Nemtin: *Mysterium*
- Karlheinz Stockhausen: *Helicopter String Quartet*
- Bull of Heaven: *310: ΩΣPxo(2^ 18×5^ 18)p*k*k*k*
- Arnold Schoenberg: Five Pieces for Orchestra, op. 16

72

Brevity

Beethoven's Bagatelle in A major, op. 119 no. 10, *Allegra-mente*: a piece whose title takes pretty much as long to say as the music does to hear. This Bagatelle is just ten seconds long, but there's a lot going on in it. It's a complete, fully fledged piece, in three parts, which sustains an interplay between syncopated rhythm and large-scale – seriously! – harmonic expectation, deferment and fulfilment, staging a battle between a secondary dominant, dominant and tonic chord – B major, E major and A major – which is only properly resolved in terms of both rhythm and harmony in its very last note. There's something absurd about cramming so much musical information into so short a musical space-time. And that's the real existential trick that Beethoven is playing on us and his pianists: to make a musical joke, to make so many points and express so many ideas in such a tiny shard of a piece.

What is it about musical brevity? Why do it? Why write pieces that are so small that some of them can be played in less than the time it takes for Usain Bolt to run a hundred metres? How – and why – have composers made music on the smallest scale? And how do they create full-size musical experiences in terms of range, emotion, expressiveness, poetry and everything else we ask of our music, within the pint-sized scale of music that lasts less than sixty seconds?

Mind you, Beethoven is positively long-form compared to James Whitehead – the artist known as JLIAT – who has attempted to compose *The Shortest Piece of Music*. This is a work that confuses most CD players on the planet, because it lasts the smallest atom of time that's technically possible using the digital sampling rate at which music is often recorded, 44,100 times a second. James's idea was to make a CD player reproduce a sound that lasts a 44,100th of a second. It can't really do it, and we can't really hear it. Our puny ears can't get down to those infinitesimal timescales, even if we're hearing aggregates of those units of time every time we hear music on a CD, which is simply millions, billions of units of 1/44,100th of a second piled up next to one another.

Yet there are whole genres that rely on brevity to make their point. Like the music of Carl Stalling, who composed scores for *Looney Tunes* cartoons. And when you hear music like Stalling's 'Wind-Up Doll' – a cue lasting forty-six seconds, originally composed for Bugs Bunny, as a sequence of sounds without the images – you hear a real orchestral tone-poem on a tiny scale, which sends up Stravinsky's ballet *Petrushka* by mangling a quotation from it. There's also time for a sentimental violin line, a drum roll, a piano solo, and a question mark of an ending. Stalling proves a point about all composer-explorers of musical brevity – just like Usain Bolt, they can't afford to put a foot wrong.

And what goes for Stalling, Beethoven and Whitehead is also true for John Zorn, Mike Patton, Judith Weir, György Kurtág, Napalm Death, J. S. Bach, Anton Webern, Frédéric Chopin, John Cage and many more. You can hear thirty complete pieces if you listen to the half-hour of the whole programme, I promise.

- ◀ Carl Stalling: 'Wind-Up Doll'
- ◀ Ludwig van Beethoven: Bagatelle in A major, op. 119 no. 10
- ◀ Judith Weir: *Mountain Airs*, part 3
- ◀ Pierre Boulez: *Notations*, no. 2
- ◀ John Zorn: 'Obeah Man', from *Naked City*

73

Martin Luther's revolution

We sing together: that's what we do as human beings, in praise of everything from God to our football teams. But where did this idea of communal singing, especially in religious contexts, come from in modern Europe?

It seems so natural to us, but communal singing was once a radical, revolutionary idea that brought religion and politics together. That's thanks to the religious reforms of Martin Luther in sixteenth-century Germany. Luther realised that when we sing together, we're doing much more than making music with each other. From church to pub – and everything in between – when we sing we're expressing identity, spirituality and solidarity. If it's a national anthem, we're singing a song that says our lot is better than your lot; if we're singing as part of a religious service, we're sometimes singing about how our version of God is better than yours – whether that's the Almighty, or, if you're at Anfield stadium in Liverpool, the divine force of Steven Gerrard.

'You'll Never Walk Alone' is sung before every match that Liverpool Football Club plays. And it's not as flippant as it seems to compare Luther's hymns to a football terrace song, because the ritual that Liverpool fans go through every time their team plays has turned that melody and those words from

Rodgers and Hammerstein's musical *Carousel* into something much more than a signature tune for a football club.

Since the early 1960s, when Liverpool adopted it as their sonic mascot, this song has gone on accruing memories and meanings every time it's sung. As well as being a call to collective identity, 'You'll Never Walk Alone' is also the fans' hymn to the comrades they lost in the Hillsborough tragedy in 1989: their singing makes a memorial bridge to departed friends and family. It's a football chant, of course – but 'You'll Never Walk Alone' at Anfield is just about the closest that football songs get to spiritual experience.

Which is how Liverpool fans are re-enacting the revolutionary values of active, engaged and transformational communal singing that Luther mobilised as an essential part of the Reformation in Germany. Among Luther's most revolutionary ideas was his use of music. Luther's own chorales – his words and tunes, like 'Ein feste Burg ist unser Gott' – were easy-to-learn melodies mapped on to words that would inspire religious devotion and imitation. And they were meant for everyone to sing. They were often based on folk tunes and farming work-songs as well as Gregorian chants, which Luther cunningly brought into his church. The idea was that you would be brought into the new church by the collective power and experience of song, so that there would be no difference between the communality of singing and the experience of religious togetherness and transcendence.

Communal singing in the service of spiritual connection and communion has come a long way since Martin Luther's time. But whether it's J. S. Bach's Passions or gospel singing, whether it's contemporary hymn-singing or chanting on football terraces, the essential meanings of the experience remain. To sing together is to make the connections and relationships between us – usually invisible, and inaudible – resound. Whether it makes us think about heaven and eternity, a lost loved one, or prepares us for the sporting or spiritual battle to come, Luther's magic fire still burns with an essential truth: when we sing together, we're not alone.

◀ Liverpool Football Club fans at Anfield: 'You'll Never Walk Alone' (Rodgers and Hammerstein)
◀ Martin Luther: 'Ein feste Burg ist unser Gott'
◀ Johann Sebastian Bach: Cantata BWV 4, *Christ lag in Todesbanden*
◀ Rev. C. J. Johnson: 'I Wanna Go Where Jesus Is'
◀ Hubert Parry: 'Jerusalem'

74

The cowpat controversy

There in the fields, where the brooks burble and the meadows hum with floral and faunal fecundity, there is a faint but glorious music to be heard, blowing quietly through the spinneys and hedgerows: a halo of folky-wolky melodies that hovers above that bucolic herd of Jersey creamers in your favourite pasture in the lower field where the drainage has always been a bit of a problem; walking, lowing madeleines of summer holidays and wheatfields where once we used to plough: ah England! Creamy, shrubbery, cowpatty England! . . .

. . . which pastoral parody echoes 'the cowpat school' of musical composition. There's a specific moment and context when the 'cowpat school' term was coined: at the Dartington Summer School in the 1950s, the brilliant – and brilliantly acerbic – composer Elisabeth Lutyens gave a talk in which she lumped Vaughan Williams and many of his contemporaries together in the music-historical pat-pile (including the 'folky-wolky melodies' line – that's Lutyens, too). She was making a distinction between the bracing modernist energy that the post-war musical world needed, which is what her music was all about, and what she thought of as the thin pottage of nostalgia, sentimentality and reheated Romanticism that she and many others felt – and some still feel – characterises

214

music by everyone from Ivor Gurney to George Butterworth, from Arnold Bax to John Ireland, from Frederick Delius to Gustav Holst.

Yet it's possible to strip away the three main things that I think Lutyens was on about in her 'cowpat' criticism: the supposed pastoralism, small 'c' conservatism and parochialism of so much early-twentieth-century British music. There's the idea that its pastoralism is pure nostalgia, mired in an eddy of musical regression. Ralph Vaughan Williams's 'Pastoral' Symphony shows us that's not true: this symphony's four movements are made of music born of his experience in the First World War. This music is a devastating confrontation with loss, and a demonstration of the creative power that can be found in grief, a catharsis and a consolation. In the way it moves and the sounds it makes, this piece is also a new kind of symphony, structurally, harmonically, expressively. Far from dead-eyed nostalgia, the 'Pastoral' Symphony is one of the most blazingly visionary utterances of the twentieth or any other century.

Conservatism? Listen to the opening of Arnold Bax's Second Symphony for a corrective to that one, and hear harmonies that are like a mix of Scriabin and Debussy, with orchestration unlike anyone else's: there are icy tremulations of violas, cellos and bassoons; a kind of dragon's sigh, before this awesome creature looks up to the heights and spits out an awesome and austere declamation in the cor anglais, clarinets and bassoon, over a weird skirl in the piano. And for an answer to the parochialism, listen to Frederick Delius's music, a sensual, cosmopolitan mix of influences from his experiences in Florida, Leipzig and Paris.

So don't believe the clichés of the cowpat: celebrate instead the diversity, the radicalism, the modernity of the composers formerly known as cowpat who should instead be known as early-modern essentials. Less catchy, but more accurate: there are whole repertoires of these vivid, internationalist anti-pastorals to be discovered. They are part of the history of British music, and they are among the most striking achievements of early-twentieth-century creativity.

- ◀ Gustav Holst: *Brook Green Suite*
- ◀ Ivor Gurney: *Ludlow and Teme*
- ◀ Ralph Vaughan Williams: Symphony no. 3, 'Pastoral'
- ◀ Arnold Bax: Symphony no. 2
- ◀ Frederick Delius: Double Concerto for violin, cello and orchestra

A CONSTELLATION OF COMPOSERS AND THEIR WORKS: WHAT THEY'VE DONE, AND HOW THEY DO IT

75

How to compose music

How do they do it? Those great composers, sitting up there on their clouds of genius? So unlike the rest of us in talent and training and divinely granted gifts; how do they come up with their symphonies, their albums, their songs, their operas? It must be as one of their number describes: David Byrne, founder of Talking Heads, creative catalyst across genres and decades, has this to say about the process of composition:

> The accepted narrative suggests that a classical composer gets a strange look in his or her eye and begins furiously scribbling a fully realised composition that couldn't exist in any other form. Or that the rock and roll singer is driven by desire and demons, and out bursts this amazing, perfectly shaped song that had to be three minutes and twelve seconds – nothing more, nothing less.

And yet: 'I think', David says, 'the path of creation is almost 180 degrees from this model.'

He's right. In fact, so opposite is the process, that you or I can do it. And you've been doing it for hours of every day of your life: using sounds in unique combinations to communicate what you're feeling in a variety of different contexts, from going shopping to talking to your family. The way you use your voice is an exquisitely sophisticated lifelong improvisation in sound and meaning. But you wouldn't call it 'composing', would you? And it's on a different level to what those composers, like Byrne, Wolfgang Mozart or Judith Weir are up to, isn't it?

No – it's not. Take the Prelude in C major from J. S. Bach's *Well-Tempered Clavier*, Book 1. It's a beautiful chain of arpeggios, a technique that any amateur pianist learns. And if you can arpeggiate, you too can create your own prelude. Or how about Mozart's D minor Fantasy for solo piano, K397? This isn't a hard piece to listen to, and it's not that hard to compose. Seriously: Mozart wasn't in a reverie of transcendence when he wrote this down. Instead he sat at the piano, and improvised a sequence of common-or-garden musical ideas – he just put them together in new ways. And you can do that too.

The Northern Irish composer Brian Irvine puts it like this: all you need to be a composer is 'a sense of curiosity about sound'. And Brian should know, because he has spent a lifetime turning groups of people who had never previously thought of themselves that way into composers. The gap between 'them' – those composers, especially 'classical' composers – and the 'us', who aren't, is a pernicious one, because it says that musical creation belongs to some other, unknowable realm that you need special tools to access. But you don't: start repeating the last sentence you just said, turn it into a tune – and you're composing, manipulating the stuff of sound in the same fundamental way that Beethoven or Brian Irvine do. We're all composers, if only we're allowed to realise it.

- Johann Sebastian Bach: Prelude in C major, BWV 846, from *The Well-Tempered Clavier*, Book 1
- David Byrne: *High Life for Nine Instruments*
- Wolfgang Amadé Mozart: Fantasia in D minor for solo piano, K397
- Cornelius Cardew: 'Paragraph 7', from *The Great Learning*
- Brian Irvine: 'Just Cut 'em Up Like Regular Chickens?', from *Montana Strange*

76

Beginnings

It's one of the key decisions that any composer in any genre has to make: how do you start a piece of music? With a call to attention, a high-octane cue that your listeners should get their ears in gear for what's going to happen next; a gesture that commands you: listen to this! That's what the fanfares and whipcracks of energy in Monteverdi's *L'Orfeo* or Mahler's Second Symphony are all about; or maybe you set out your stall with the ideas and themes you're going to develop in the piece, like an operatic overture, from Verdi's *La traviata* to Rossini's *William Tell*. Or you can begin in a state of mysterious becoming, where nothing is formed yet; a state of suspense until you unleash something more definite: Mahler's First Symphony, Beethoven's Ninth and Haydn's oratorio *The Creation* are all in that category of ear-tickling and soul-trembling anticipation.

It's hard enough for composers of instrumental music and opera from the seventeenth to the nineteenth centuries, but musicians in the twenty-first century have an even greater challenge to grab our attention with the way their music starts. Research suggests that there's a three-second rule that our brains are hard-wired with: entertain us in the first three seconds, otherwise we're going to switch off and find something more interesting instead. That means there's more at stake at the start of piece of music than at any other point in its structure. If you can't hook us in at the start, we're lost as listeners, and you've lost as a composer.

Today, composers and musicians have got to compete against the continual online availability of the entire musical history of humanity as we dive into a world of endless digital streaming, so the start of your new song or symphony has got to be pretty special if it's going to stand a chance of us listening until the end of the track or movement, let alone to the whole piece or album. If we're not into it after three seconds, we'll have swiped right on to the next track. That's one reason that the art of the long intro in pop songs in particular has largely been lost to the mists of time, to prog-rock and ambient history: in the age of streaming, songs are getting shorter, and they get straight to the point, right to the hook, instead of indulging in minutes of moody set-up, as Dire Straits could do in the 1980s in a track like 'Money for Nothing'. It's not only that we want MTV – as Sting dreamily sings in the epic intro to that eight-and-a-half-minute track – we've now got Spotify, Tidal, and all the rest, and our three seconds of attention have the whole of musical history to choose from, so you can't hang around any more: entertain us! Quickly!

There are correctives to this culture of endless beginnings in which we trap ourselves, at either end of the spectrum: if you've only got three seconds, why not write a three-second song, complete in itself? Death metal bands like Napalm Death have done exactly that; and if we can get past our ingrained three-second rule, the time-stopping opening of Wagner's *Ring* cycle – a single E flat major chord sustained for five minutes, flowing through the orchestra, a creation of a new kind of time, appropriate for the start of a sixteen-hour music-dramatic cycle – is a very good place to start.

These musical beginnings belie the fact that every song, symphony or any other piece of music that we choose to hear is always intruding into the middle of our own listening, which isn't actually bounded by the edges of pieces of music, but by the limitlessness of our own hearing – our ears and our frequency-resonating bodies don't stop and start. How do you start a piece of music? You need to get some listeners!

- ◀ Giuseppe Verdi: *La forza del destino*, Overture
- ◀ Anna Meredith: *Nautilus*
- ◀ Joseph Haydn: *The Creation*, Overture – 'The Representation of Chaos'
- ◀ David Bowie: 'Heroes', from *Christiane F.*
- ◀ Louis Armstrong: 'West End Blues'

77

Endings

Crash, bang, wallop: what an ending! The sounds of the conclusions to many pieces of classical orchestral music are strikingly similar: massively loud and massively fast build-ups of excitement towards a final cadence, the cue for applause in the audience and for musical closure. These familiar gestures connect Mozart's 'Jupiter' Symphony to Beethoven's Eighth, Tchaikovsky's Fourth to Beethoven's Second, Elgar's Cello Concerto to Schumann's Piano Concerto.

Whatever their differences of epoch and instrumentation, all those conclusions – and thousands more – share the same musical principle: the final affirmation of the home key of the symphony or concerto is clinched by a move towards it from a chord on the fifth degree of the scale: V–I, in music-theoretical symbology.

But what do these endings mean? How do pieces of music end? And why? Because these classical endings don't exist in the same way in other musical cultures: there's the vamp-till-ready in musical theatre; the cues that bleed into the next track in film scores; the fades into silence in pop songs; the jazz sets that cut into applause after everyone's had their solo. Those endings are like interruptions in a larger musical or social event, rather than the apocalyptic full stops of classical endings.

This kind of classical ending has a very particular meaning: it's a marker of where the world of the art-work ends, and the real world begins. The hammering conclusion of a piece like Beethoven's Fifth Symphony, with its obsessive repetitions of the same chords, insists that this piece is its own self-contained realm, separate in dimension and character from the rest of our lives. The final bars of Beethoven's Fifth Symphony sound like the end of a world – because that's exactly what they are.

The conductor Colin Davis said that he felt that the ends of his performances were existential moments: the last chord of every concert a question of life and death.

Many composers have made music from that idea, so that the end of a symphony, an opera, a string quartet, is explicitly about death and dying, as in the final slow movements, leave-takings of the world, in Tchaikovsky's 'Pathétique' Symphony or Mahler's Ninth. The ends of pieces are rehearsals for the end of the universe.

The latest idea about the sounds of the heat-death of the universe, trillions of years in the future, is that the energy of the biggest black holes will dissipate into the vastly empty ether, and the noise of the final moments of these mighty engines of galactic creation and destruction will be a medium-sized pop rather than an apocalyptic explosion. Everything will just stop. No frame, no gesture – just the end.

Johann Sebastian Bach's *Art of Fugue* was unfinished at his death: the polyphony of Contrapunctus 14 may have been among the last notes he composed. The manuscript runs out just after Bach wrote a musical line that uses his musical moniker (B–A–C–H is translated into B flat–A–C–B natural, using the German system of note-names). He signs out, in one of the voices in the fugue – and then the music just stops. Maybe Bach knew what was coming: not just in our lives, but the fate of all things.

- Ludwig van Beethoven: Symphony no. 5 in C minor, op. 67, finale
- Joseph Haydn: Symphony no. 45 in F sharp minor, 'Farewell', finale
- Giorgio Moroder and Philip Oakey: 'Together in Electric Dreams'
- Mauricio Kagel: *Finale*
- Pyotr Ilyich Tchaikovsky: Symphony no. 6 in B minor, 'Pathétique', finale

78

Sonata form – or, There and Back Again

I've a story to tell you: Princess Hedwig has a happy home life in the fantastical medieval castle of Schloss Schwanstein, which she has to leave to embark on a heroic quest to rescue her prince, Ludwig, from the clutches of a ferocious dragon. On the way, she encounters former lovers, helpful peasants and clownish aristocrats, before rescuing Ludwig after a titanic clash of *Homo sapiens* against the reptile king, bringing her prince home on her flying steed. The End.

A terrible story, I hope you'll agree, but what I've just done is create a micro-narrative that had three main parts: what I'm going to call an exposition – the establishment of Hedwig's home life; a development – her questing search for Ludwig; and a recapitulation – her victory against the dragon and their return home, all resolved. Even more succinctly, it's a story of 'There and Back Again', as J. R. R. Tolkien's Bilbo Baggins puts it.

In miniature, that was a story in 'sonata form': and for all its forbidding formalism and those quotation marks, sonata form isn't a remote structural concept. Instead, for music of the eighteenth and nineteenth centuries, sonata form is a gateway onto new ways of feeling and experiencing what the artform can do.

During the middle of the eighteenth century, something happened in the way that music was composed for instruments. In the earlier part of the century, the idea was to explore the emotional and musical world of each musical and emotional idea, one at a time. That's why J. S. Bach's preludes and fugues, and the movements of his suites or partitas, have an emotional temperature that remains reasonably constant from their beginning to their end. Sad pieces stay sad, happy ones happy.

But in pieces using what became known as sonata form (though not until Anton Reicha coined the term in 1824, around seventy years after composers had begun working with it), there is instead a law of contrasts at work: contrasts of character, emotion and feeling. Sonata form structures and experiences – whether we're hearing them in a Beethoven symphony, a Haydn string quartet or a Schubert sonata – have an engine of musical and dramatic friction at their heart, in their journeys away from a home key and back again. We encounter different themes with different characters, which generate drama in the way they conflict with one another.

In fact, so much classical music works in this way that it's not just pieces of music that are cast in sonata form, but our mode of listening to music. Our ears now expect a sonata-like journey of home–away–resolution, of there and back again, similar to the dramatic arc we look for in our novels, films, and the narrative maps that we create for our lives.

Hold on: I think I'm saying that we might live our lives in sonata form; in symphonies of discovering and struggling against the world, only to return to the things we thought we knew – the home, the people, the relationships – renewed by the journey. Sonata form isn't just a musical metaphor: it's a generating principle for how we live our lives.

- ◀ Kurt Schwertsik: *Shrunken Symphony*, op. 80, first movement
- ◀ Johannes Brahms: Symphony no. 3 in F major, op. 90, first movement
- ◀ Anton Bruckner: Symphony no. 6 in A major, first movement
- ◀ Pierre Boulez: Piano Sonata no. 2, first movement
- ◀ Thomas Adès: Piano Quintet

79

Style counsel

We are all acutely sensitive to musical styles. If I play some genteel baroque harpsichord music to you, you might be plunged in your imagination into a period drama; some surging Romantic orchestral music suggests a passionate lovers' tryst in a Hollywood movie; while acerbically dissonant electronica might conjure up a post-apocalyptic sci-fi doomscape.

Your images and associations may differ, but musical styles can be an amazingly powerful expressive shorthand, which film and TV composers are especially adept at exploiting. But all composers do it. What do these styles mean, and why do they mean what they do?

The Associated Board of the Royal Schools of Music has some handy style guides for historical stylistic identification: eighteenth-century baroque music is made of a combination of polyphony and strong cadences as well as elaborate ornamentation; the rococo style is simpler, with an emphasis on tunes and accompaniments, like Mozart's music; moving on to the luxuriant orchestration and richer harmonies of nineteenth-century Romanticism, and the unpredictable rhythms and harmonies of twentieth-century modernism. Historical styles, codified and clarified.

But reducing centuries of music to a few clichéd techniques only gets you so far in describing the relationship between the style of a piece of music and what the composer is really trying to communicate. Composers from Mozart to Tchaikovsky were never composing only to fill out the conventions of a style, but to express something new and urgent in every piece they wrote.

Fast-forward to the twenty-first century and the styles just keep on multiplying, across every genre you can imagine – from minimalism to post-modernism, from free improvisation to grime. So what would a music of this information-saturated world sound like? The American composer John Zorn's *Carny* is a good answer. It's a solo piano piece that gives the lie to the idea that a musical work ought to be cast in a single style. Zorn quotes shards of music by Karlheinz Stockhausen, Béla Bartók and Charles Ives, as well earlier classical styles, jazz, bebop and cartoon scores, alongside newly composed material, jump-cutting from one to the other every few seconds. This is a piece that answers that question about what you do when every style is available to you, with a response that style really doesn't matter.

Carny is music that's about an ever-changing dynamism: not the styles themselves but the unpredictable cutting from one to another. And it's a piece that proves that what's important in composition isn't what style your material is in – it's how you combine and recombine all of these shards of musical existence that counts.

It's not only Zorn: pieces by composers from Igor Stravinsky to Ludwig van Beethoven demonstrate the same truth, that styles exist only as arbitrary categories, as pigeonholes that narrow and constrict musical imagination. Styles are a starting point for musical composition, not its goal. It ain't what you've got, it's what you do with it that really matters.

- John Zorn: *Carny*
- Igor Stravinsky: *Pulcinella*
- Ludwig van Beethoven: Bagatelle in F major, op. 33 no. 3
- Pyotr Ilyich Tchaikovsky: Piano Concerto no. 1 in B flat minor, third movement
- Wolfgang Amadé Mozart: Piano Sonata no. 16 in C major, K545, first movement

80

Chasing a fugue

Why do we all need fugues in our lives? Because the pleasure of listening to the most dazzling fugues – by Bach, Beethoven or Bruckner – is to throw your ears into a dazzling kaleidoscopic play of multi-voiced musical possibility. They're multi-dimensional musical weavings of time and space that are all about a love for counterpoint, in which composers use the inspiration of a simple initial idea – the 'subject', the first melody you hear on its own, which nearly every fugue must have – to create a labyrinthine web of musical lines.

'Fugue'? 'Counterpoint'? Don't think you've sung them, understood them? You have: all you need to remember is how you sing a tune like 'London Bridge is Falling Down, Falling Down, Falling Down', as each voice loops the melody against itself. 'London Bridge' is a round, or to use a more arcane term, a 'canon' – which means the same tune repeated against itself, starting at different times. And that's also a rudimentary form of counterpoint – which means simply one voice, literally in this case, against another, and another.

And in those rounds and canons we all sing, there's an essential connection with the idea of the fugue. The relationship between the round and the fugue is implicit in a bit of music-historical etymology, because the word 'fugue' has one of

234

its roots in the Latin *fugare*, 'to chase'. The subject of a fugue – like the only melody of a round or a canon – chases itself throughout the work's structure. In a fugue like the five-voice edifice of orchestral and choral counterpoint in the 'Kyrie' of Bach's Mass in B minor, the same melody appears in different registers, from the bass voices to the sopranos, starting on different notes. Yet for all the complexity of the labyrinth that Bach creates from this melody, its identity doesn't change: it's still the same tune, chasing itself through a musical maze of its own construction.

The difference between a 'round' and a 'fugue' is one of freedom: in a piece called 'fugue', you're liable to hear a much freer, more improvisational kind of composition, full of unpredictable developments and fantastical interruptions of character, idea and imagination. It's up to the composer to decide how many voices we're going to hear, which keys we go through, how long the piece is, what its drama is going to be.

Fugues might have reached, for many, an unassailable high point with J. S. Bach, and if I had to choose one fugal composition to sum up his outrageous virtuosity of contrapuntal thinking and overwhelming emotional power, it would be his six-voice Ricercar from *The Musical Offering*: six co-dependent musical lines simultaneously creating their own thread of time through the fugue-osphere, based on a fugal improvisation that Bach came up with on a tune suggested by Frederick the Great in 1747.

Yet fugues never really went out of fashion. Haydn, Mozart and Beethoven all prove themselves with their fugues, and so do Mendelssohn and Farrenc, Brahms and Mahler. And fugues are a form made for the digital technologies of the twenty-first century, for the age of YouTube and big-musical-data visualisation. You can watch the tangled lines of Bach's *Art of Fugue* unfold in front of your eyes as well as your ears, in different dimensions of colour and illustration, and watch scores go by as you listen, all illustrated with live fugal analysis. Don't be frightened of the fugue: dive into the contrapuntal labyrinth and enjoy some of the most vertiginous rides of musical imagination that composers have ever created.

- ◀ Johann Sebastian Bach: 'Ricercar à 6' from *The Musical Offering*
- ◀ John Lewis: 'A Fugue for Music Inn' (The Modern Jazz Quartet)
- ◀ Dmitri Shostakovich: Prelude and Fugue in A minor, op. 87 no. 2
- ◀ Anton Bruckner: Symphony no. 5 in B flat major, finale
- ◀ Giovanni Dettori: 'Lady Gaga Fugue'

81

The joy of Bach

Johann Sebastian Bach: clever, wasn't he? His music's the very acme of musical seriousness, isn't it? In fact, it's not just clever in a normal human sense: Bach was a multi-dimensional genius of a composer and spiritual thinker. He wrote fugues that collapse musical time and space; and he composed choral pieces that meditate on multiple musical layers simultaneously to tell a story that's both personal and universal: the *St John* and *St Matthew* Passions, which mediate between the public and the private, the intellectual and the spiritual.

As the East German author Wolf Biermann said: 'I don't believe in God, but I do believe in Bach.' Case closed – we shouldn't listen to Bach, we should worship him for creating these perfected musical-spiritual visions.

But I think we should get up from our genuflectory postures when we listen to Bach. Because Bach only accesses that world of the numinous through our bodies, through the sensuality and pleasure that his music can give us. Instead of the seriousness, we should be transported by the life-giving joy of Bach's music.

Bach made his music from a delight in his own corporeally joyful virtuosity. His particular obsession was all the keyboard instruments he could get his hands on in the early eighteenth century: the harpsichord, the clavichord, the fortepiano, and above all, the organ. As an organist, Bach was an improviser, for whom the instrument was a cosmic infinity of musical possibility. The pieces he composed as a young musician are wildly, dazzlingly virtuosic and experimental. The G major Fantasia and the Toccata and Fugue in D minor are written-down versions of music that came to Bach on the wings of in-the-moment fantasy. It's music made to show off his presti-digitatory, improvisational chops.

There are the meditative joys of his cantatas, there's the dancing delirium of his Brandenburg Concertos, and even the joyful flights of pure compositional fantasy of his counter-point and canons, as in his unfinished assemblage of creative possibility, *The Art of Fugue*.

But the deep joy of Bach's music is the way it creates a community of participation. It's designed to make our bodies exquisitely sympathetic resonators of the feelings the music creates, as well as to prime our minds and our intellects. It makes all our human faculties work in concert with each other, so that the community we make when we listen to Bach – the relationship between composer, performers and audiences – is a collective social and spiritual transaction. There's no better example of that alchemy in action than a performance that John Butt conducted with the Dunedin Consort at the BBC Proms in the summer of 2017, in which the audience became a singing congregation, and the piece was returned to the fabric of the life of the liturgy, so that it spoke across dimensions of space, and time. What's the joy of Bach? Nothing less than the joy of being fully alive.

Johann Sebastian Bach

◀ *St John Passion*: chorus, 'Herr, unser Herrscher'
◀ Mass in B minor: Gloria
◀ Fugue in C minor for organ, BWV 537
◀ *Christmas Oratorio*, Cantata 1: 'Jauchzet, frohlocket!'
◀ *The Art of Fugue*: Contrapunctus 9, *alla duodecima*

82

Bach's Goldberg Variations

Just what are Bach's Goldberg Variations? On its title page, this piece was called a *Clavier-übung* – a keyboard practice or education – 'consisting of an aria with diverse variations, for the harpsichord with two manuals'. There are thirty variations in the Goldbergs on the Aria, which is repeated at the end of the piece. That means there are thirty-two pieces of music in total in the Goldberg Variations – and each piece is made of thirty-two bars. They are all based on the same bass-line, which is shared by everything from the meditative serenity of the Aria, to the gigantic energy and contrapuntal complexity of Variation 28 and the Quodlibet, a medley of tunes piled on top of one another, which Bach composes as the thirtieth variation.

The exquisite pain of Variation 25 proves the astonishing expressive extremes that Bach finds within the frames of his geometric limitations. In G minor, it's a movement that the harpsichordist Wanda Landowska called the 'black pearl' of the Goldbergs, and it writhes in a constant chromatic torpor. It's the dark underside of the gentleness of the opening aria: each note feels like a corporeal mutilation of that innocent bass-line. And the emotional darkness of this variation is more devastating because for all the nihilism we might feel in it, it's made of the same stuff – the same number of bars, the same bass-line – as all the others. Bach's processes and systems and structures are fully in operation: so what we experience isn't a subjective, heart-on-sleeve emotion that can be explained through storyline, heartbreak or plot twist, but something much deeper: a point of devastation reached by the system itself, an unsentimental despair that has an objective power, independent of our agency as listeners or even performers.

And after around eighty minutes, after all that brain-wracking, soul-cleaving energy, all that compositional craft and keyboard virtuosity, the music ends up where it began, with an exact repeat of the opening Aria. But when we hear it this second time, everything has changed. The mystery of the Goldberg Variations is completed by this final riddle: the ultimate shape of the structure of these 'diverse variations' is a perpetually repeating cycle, an eighty-minute round, which could start again, or inspire another set of more diverse variations. These uncannily brilliant variations warp time into a Möbius strip.

Why do the Goldberg Variations fascinate us so much? Because they are a mirror for some of the deep truths about who we are as a species. The same structure, diversely varied: that's a pretty good description of our biology, of the similarities and differences between all of us as human beings. The Goldberg Variations aren't only musical DNA. In how we experience them, in the way the music inserts itself not only into our souls but into our cells, this music is a writing-out of the principles of creation that govern the atoms of our bodies and all of the scales of life in between the shape of us and the shape of the universe.

Johann Sebastian Bach: Goldberg Variations –
a selection of recordings

◀ Richard Egarr, harpsichord
◀ Glenn Gould, piano (both recordings, 1955 and 1981)
◀ Wanda Landowska, harpsichord
◀ Jeremy Denk, piano
◀ Rosalyn Tureck, piano (1999 recording)

83

Wolfgang Amadé Mozart

Four crazy myths about Mozart. And the crazier truth.

Amadeus

He almost never called himself 'Amadeus'. 'Amadeus' is a moniker – ossified since the play and film by Peter Shaffer – that confers upon him a graceless, taken-for-granted genius. 'Amadeus' is an immortal, pseudo-Latinised pedestal that his memory longs to be released from. Mozart should be returned to the 'Amadé' with which he actually signed his name: he wasn't 'Amadeus' but Wolfgang Amadé Mozart. Amadeus is the superhuman myth and the brand of posterity that binds Mozart's image to chocolate balls and tourist traps, but Amadé is the supernormal man. And that's who he really was.

He took dictation from God

He didn't: Mozart worked, hard, at everything he wrote. He was capable, like many musicians of the time, of working out a piece in his head, improvising it at the keyboard, and writing it down when he needed to. But to think of his music as an agency-free act of divine dictation robs Mozart of his humanity. He wanted his operas, like *The Marriage of Figaro* or *The*

Magic Flute, to be part of the society, the political world, and the entertainment industry of his time.

He was smuttily infantile

Mozart's scatological references in his letters, and his pieces like the canon 'Lick me in the arse', K231, seem to give credence to the image of him as someone stuck in a Peter Pan-like denial of adulthood. It's not true: his whole family and his friends were capable of virtuosic vulgarity in their letters to each other, but Mozart was a clear-sighted observer of the world. He knew how Europe was changing in his lifetime, and he wanted to be part of it. He was the first freelance musician in Vienna, putting his money and his livelihood where his mouth was, risking everything to create a new economy away from the court and the church.

He was murdered by Salieri

Amadeus is a great play, but a terrible biography. Mozart died, entirely of natural causes, on the night of 5 December 1791 at the age of thirty-five. Salieri was a supporter of his, not an enemy, and he certainly didn't poison him in a fit of mediocrity-melancholy. In fact, Mozart's last year puts him on the path to new musical possibilities, glimpsed in the unfinished Requiem, but never realised in the life he couldn't lead.

The truth

Mozart's music is a virtuosity of empathy. His music is addressed to us, from one messily human being to another. He doesn't judge, he doesn't scorn, he fearlessly accepts the crazy condition of humanity, and rejoices in it.

Wolfgang Amadé Mozart

◀ Symphony no. 29 in A major, K201
◀ String Quartet no. 14 in G major, K387
◀ *Don Giovanni*
◀ Symphony no. 41 in C major, K551, 'Jupiter'
◀ Piano Concerto no. 27 in B flat major, K595

84

Beethoven: hero or villain?

Was Beethoven a hero? Or was he a villain? Here's the problem. Beethoven's complete, all-conquering heroism has made it difficult for any other subsequent composer to come close to him. We tell the story of his life as a heroic narrative of conquering his deafness to storm the heavens in his music; and we say that his works themselves are victories over fate, from the literally heroic 'Eroica' symphony to the darkness-to-light arrow of time that is the Fifth Symphony, or the hard-won 'Ode to Joy' of the Ninth.

Which means it's as if every subsequent composer is living in Beethoven's shadow: no one can measure up to Ludwig, the original and best musical hero. Here goes for a clichéd summary of Beethoven's followers in the later nineteenth century. Johannes Brahms? His First Symphony could only be heard as Beethoven's Tenth – how can you compose, Brahms said, with that giant on your shoulders? Felix Mendelssohn? Not nearly heroic enough: too fluid, too lyrical, no revolution. Robert Schumann? A dreamer, not a doer. Frédéric Chopin? Sentimental indulgence, and a miniaturist, to boot. Anton Bruckner basically rewrote Beethoven's Ninth Symphony over and over again; Richard Wagner rewrote history to make it seem as if his was the only true continuation of Beethoven's work in his music dramas, but he completely ducked the challenge of following him in instrumental music.

But before we start pitying other composers, we should pity Beethoven himself. Because if we value his music only for its fate-conquering 'heroism', we're going to miss out on the other qualities of the vast majority of the music he wrote: the lyricism and strangeness of his Bagatelles for solo piano, the inwardness of his only song-cycle, *An die ferne Geliebte*, or the beguiling sensuousness of the 'Harp' Quartet, op. 74.

And the nature-infatuated reverie of his Sixth Symphony, the 'Pastoral'. The way the climaxes are made in this symphony – especially in the first and last movements – achieves an ecstasy of becoming, rather than a single longed-for moment of glory. Instead of promises of world-changing utopian deeds like the Fifth and Ninth Symphonies, this piece is about the consolations of repetition, and of compassion, of oneness with the world rather than dominion over it.

Scott Burnham ends his book *Beethoven Hero* by saying that instead of confining ourselves – and him – to this single heroic conception, we should escape into 'the dangerous promise of an open sea' that's not bounded by those dominating problematic musical heroics. He says that we should 'interact with music in ways that speak of human identities as broadly conceived as the world is wide. And this is how we may best continue to honor Beethoven . . . by staying in touch with the hero within ourselves, the hero whose presence is music.' So instead of that tarnished one-dimensional heroism, let's hear it for all of his music – and let's hear it for Beethoven, Anti-Hero.

Ludwig van Beethoven

◀ Symphony no. 5 in C minor, op. 67, first movement
◀ Piano Sonata no. 24 in F sharp major, op. 78
◀ *An die ferne Geliebte* (song-cycle)
◀ Symphony no. 6 in F major, op. 68, 'Pastoral': final movement, 'Shepherd's Song. Cheerful and thankful feelings after the storm'
◀ *Für Elise* for solo piano, WoO 59

85

Beethoven's Ninth Symphony

Is the finale of Beethoven's Ninth Symphony the most dangerous piece of music ever written? Is the tune at its heart, the 'Ode to Joy', setting Schiller's words, something to be afraid of? In 1824, a choir had never previously been heard in a symphony, and the composer Louis Spohr thought the Ninth's last movement was disturbing, perverted, and that the 'Ode to Joy' tune was 'monstrous . . . tasteless'. Fanny Mendelssohn also hated the finale, calling it 'abominable' and 'burlesque'. For the harpsichordist Gustav Leonhardt in the twentieth century, the 'Ode to Joy' melody was simply 'puerile'.

But the 'Ode to Joy' is one of the most utopian tunes ever composed in Western history: Beethoven's melody, setting Schiller's text, makes it a hymn to universal fraternity. Yet the 'Ode to Joy' has also been used and abused: as a powerful symbol for dictatorships, like the Third Reich; as an anthem for racist nation states, like Rhodesia; and as the accompaniment to ultra-violence in Stanley Kubrick's *A Clockwork Orange*, in which the anti-hero Alex is inspired by Wendy Carlos's electronic version of the Ninth. As Jan Swafford says in his biography, *Beethoven: Anguish and Triumph*: 'how one views the Ninth . . . depended on what kind of Elysium one had in mind, whether all people should be brothers or that all non-brothers should be exterminated'.

In 1989, the Ninth Symphony was played as an 'Ode to Freedom' (*Freiheit* – 'freedom' – was substituted for the original word *Freude*, or 'joy') in a performance conducted by Leonard Bernstein to mark the fall of the Berlin Wall. Yet in the same city, on Hitler's birthday in 1942, you could have heard and seen a performance by the *Reichsorchester*, the Berlin Philharmonic, conducted with demonic energy by Wilhelm Furtwängler. This might be the single most intense and awesome performance in the history of the piece, yet the circumstances that produced it are chilling. Is its extremity intended as a fist in the face of the Nazis who applaud it, including Joseph Goebbels, who shakes Furtwängler's hand at the end, as you can see in the film of this very performance? Or is it rather Furtwängler's realisation of what the piece is to him: his gift to the watching and listening millions on German radio? What does it mean to celebrate the musical value of this performance, to listen to it on its own terms – if that means not acknowledging the context around it?

Yet it's precisely these dangers that mean we still need the Ninth. The fact that this tune has been so many things to so many people – for better, and so often, for worse – means we must attend to the Ninth Symphony as an endlessly contemporary piece. Beethoven doesn't actually realise utopia in his music: if he had done, our societies would look a whole lot different to the way they do now. He doesn't give us a political and social brotherhood that we can really live in. Instead, the question of how we interpret the exhilarating experience at the end of the piece is up to us: whether we treat it merely as a thunderingly thrilling noise, or whether it makes us want to question our dreams and destinies as individuals and as societies. After almost two centuries, Beethoven's Ninth is still an unanswered question – and that's why we have to keep returning to it. However terrifying the places it takes us to, the questions it forces us to ask about who we are, about the power of music, about the tyranny and the transcendence of joy, have never been more urgent.

Ludwig van Beethoven: Symphony no. 9 in D minor, op. 125:

◀ Wilhelm Furtwängler/Berlin Philharmonic Orchestra (April 1942, Berlin)
◀ Leonard Bernstein/musicians from Germany, Britain, America, Russia, France (December 1989, Berlin)
◀ Riccardo Chailly/Leipzig Gewandhaus Orchestra (2011)
◀ Paul Robeson: 'Ode to Joy'
◀ Wendy Carlos: music from *A Clockwork Orange*

86

Schubert – the dark side

I know the moment it really hit me: when I realised that Franz Schubert wasn't the little mushroom man of lovelorn adolescent cheeriness; and I say 'little mushroom' because that's what his friends patronisingly called him – *Schwammerl*, in Viennese dialect. With his diminutive stature, his eyes peering out from behind those thick glasses, his fulsome physique, he might have given the impression of a wee round man from whose every pore the stuff of sweetness ought to ooze.

As it does, in many of his songs and his dances. But Schubert reveals himself more fully in a profoundly disturbing piano sonata in A minor he composed in 1823, when he was twenty-six. I tried to play this piece, and it wasn't just the difficulty of the notes that froze me, it was the atmosphere of the music. It feels like your hands are turning to ice when you play it. The first movement begins with a stark melody, without any harmony at all to hide its nakedness: it's music like a skeleton, pared down to its bones. And it's obsessive, too, in the way it returns to a gloomy semitone, over and over again, seeming to savour its dissonance and its anguish. There are fractured, wheezing chords, like an asthmatic squeeze-box, before a haunted melody tries to heave itself up into life, but it manages only to sound like a sort of musical zombie: not quite alive; tainted by the desperate atmosphere of the music around it.

Where does it come from? It's a musical expression of Schubert's realisation of the symptoms of syphilis that would kill him in 1828, at the age of just thirty-one, but it's also music that reflects this composer's ambition. Schubert's music isn't about resolving the conflicts of darkness and light, pleasure and pain, despair and joy – in the way that Beethoven's music often tries to do. Instead, Schubert's music is a fearless revelation that both extremes of experience must always exist, and that this duality must be accepted as the essence of our lives.

Schubert's close friend Joseph Kenner described him like this: 'He was made of two natures . . . [his] body, strong as it was, succumbed to the cleavage in his souls . . . of which one pressed heavenwards and the other bathed in slime.' In his music, that means sudden and extreme juxtapositions of blinding light and harrowing, screaming anguish, as in the storm that erupts without warning in the middle of the slow movement of his A major piano sonata, D959.

Schubert's brilliance is to be honest enough to put every aspect of his riven personality on the line in his music, and to allow the rest of us to hear our own natures resound with him and his music in sympathy: the light and the darkness, the heaven and the slime.

It's no surprise to me that Schubert's music was a favourite of another fearless poet of life's miraculous futility, Samuel Beckett. And yet – like Beckett – in showing us that inescapable endgame of what we're all ultimately about, Schubert creates a music that's as essential and life-affirming and truthful as anything that's ever been written.

Franz Schubert

- ◀ 'Der Leiermann', from the song-cycle *Winterreise*
- ◀ Symphony no. 9 in C major, D944, 'The Great',
  second movement
- ◀ Piano Sonata in A minor, D784, first movement
- ◀ String Quartet no. 15 in G major, D887, first movement
- ◀ 'Die Forelle'

87

Rossini – master chef and maestro

Who was the most famous and popular composer of the early nineteenth century: Beethoven? Schubert? Mendelssohn? None of the above – the answer is the Italian composer Gioachino Rossini, the phenomenon who turned out two operas a year, who bestrode the world as the incarnation of musical popularity, thanks to the fizzing joy of music like Figaro's aria from Act 1 of *The Barber of Seville*, 'Largo al factotum'. You know the one: 'FigaroFigaroFigaro'; Figaro here, Figaro there – Figaro everywhere.

And yet something strange and troubling has happened to Rossini's reputation today. Where once he had the entire musical world in his thrall, his music and his reputation have suffered over the last century and a half since his death in November 1868.

Rossini is a victim of his own success. It's a curious quirk that while we apparently have unreserved admiration and awe for Handel churning out his oratorios in a couple of weeks, and for Mozart composing symphonies in a few days, we seem to view Rossini's facility – composing *The Barber of Seville* in a fortnight, and the other operas almost as quickly – as evidence not of preternatural genius, but rather of untrustworthy fecundity, out of step with the deeply felt Romanticism that would later grip European music. Rossini's overtures prove the point: so little did he care for dramatic unity or musical cohesion, he used the same overtures for different operas – like the one for *The Barber of Seville*, which was also the curtain-raiser to two previous shows, *Aureliano in Palmira*, and *Elisa-betta, regina d'Inghilterra*. Ridiculous, we say – at the same time forgetting that Handel, Bach, Mozart and many others were also always up to similar kinds of self-recycling. No matter: Rossini is the one who gets marked down for laziness.

It's a music-historical hypocrisy that needs correcting. I love Rossini – the music and the man. There's no need for special pleading on his behalf because it's all there in his music, from comic to serious operas to what he called the 'sins of his old age': some of the strangest and wittiest piano pieces ever composed, and the moving intimacy of his *Petite messe solennelle*.

And if you need convincing, just listen to the very last music he wrote for the theatre, before he retired from the public stage at the age of just thirty-seven. The final minutes of *William Tell* are some of the most thrilling pages in the entire operatic repertoire: a harp-strewn sunrise, a blinding vision in orchestral and vocal sound, the sunrise of a new world of liberty.

The liberty this music is suffused with is all the more moving, the more transcendent, because it's rooted in the human experience of the characters of *William Tell*, just as Rossini's music is rooted in its time and place. The world is a better place because of Rossini's music, as we sing and hum and are still obsessed by his tunes and his finales, his coloratura and his crescendos. Viva Rossini!

Gioachino Rossini

◀ 'Largo al factotum', from *The Barber of Seville*
◀ *Le Comte Ory*: Act 1 finale
◀ 'Non più mesta', from *La Cenerentola*
◀ *William Tell*: Act 4 finale
◀ 'Mon prélude hygiénique du matin', for solo piano, from *Péchés de vieillesse*

88

Brahms: behind the beard

Who was Johannes Brahms, under that stultifyingly grey beard? The face that Brahms presented to the world, especially in later life in Vienna in the 1880s and 1890s – gruff, cynical, self-deprecating, world-weary, forbidding – was a mask, or a whole series of masks, that he had made for himself throughout his life.

And those masks are still there in the way we think about Brahms's life and his music. We hear a piece like his First Symphony in C minor or the *German Requiem* and we think it's classical with a capital 'C', a late-nineteenth-century style that's all about stodgy statement rather than emotional expression. It's as if Brahms's music is the embodiment in sound of lugubrious, monumentalised, Gothic Victorian architecture: it glories in self-pitying we-aren't-worthiness rather than revelling in the unfettered possibilities of creative genius.

But what's really beneath Brahms's beard? In fact, there's an exquisite alchemy of personal torment, poetic expression and historical self-awareness which makes his music multi-dimensionally moving.

A handful of pieces prove the point. Take the opening of the First Piano Concerto in D minor, completed in 1858, when Brahms was in his mid-twenties. This piece pushes the orchestra so hard that it strains at the limits of what they can do. It's one of those musical moments that should be heard as a shock to the system – orchestral, emotional, personal, a piece that reflects Brahms's torment over the death of Robert Schumann, and the torturous reality of his love for his widow, Clara.

Or how about Brahms's choral work *The Song of the Fates*, written when he was fifty: *Gesang der Parzen*, to give it the German title, is a setting of a desperately austere poem by Goethe for chorus and orchestra, about mankind being shunned by the gods, which ends with an image of an old man, alone, in a cave. The opening of this piece is sublimely frightening. It's the same key as the D minor Piano Concerto, but here, the torment isn't merely personal, it's the impassive fury of the gods and humanity's fear of them that screams and churns within Brahms's tortured counterpoint.

On a completely different scale, there are Brahms's late piano pieces, some of the last music he wrote before his death in 1897: they're each just a few minutes long, but they compress, distil and supercharge the power of the notes he's working with, so that their melancholy, terror and consolations become ours. Brahms wrote to Clara Schumann about these pieces: 'Every bar and every note must be played as if . . . one wished to draw the melancholy out of each one of them, and voluptuous joy and comfort out of the discords.' Brahms's beard and posterity's caricature of his conservative worthiness are just masks: his music is a voluptuous, melancholic revelation of shattering worlds of feeling.

Johannes Brahms

◀ Piano Concerto no. 1 in D minor, op. 15, first movement
◀ String Sextet no. 2 in G major, op. 36, first movement
◀ *Gesang der Parzen*
◀ Intermezzo for solo piano in A major, op. 118 no. 2
◀ Symphony no. 4 in E minor, op. 98, final movement

89

Bruckner and the symphonic boa constrictors

Ah Anton: what are we going to do with you? Anton Bruckner, I mean. They said you wrote symphonic boa constrictors – or at least that's how Johannes Brahms described your symphonies. But just because Bruckner's symphonies were twice as long as yours, Johannes, there's no need to be jealous.

Another common criticism about Bruckner's music – and one of the other reasons he's a Marmite composer for so many music-lovers – is that he wrote the same symphony over and over again in his nine numbered symphonies. That's because a few of them – including the most performed pieces, the Fourth and Seventh – start with a cosmically quiet string tremolo, following the example of Beethoven's Ninth Symphony.

But in fact, the story of Bruckner's symphonic openings shows how original this composer truly is. Bruckner's Fifth starts with three weirdly dissociated ideas. There's a pizzicato tread underneath a spot of Renaissance polyphony in the strings. There's a silence – and then comes a massively loud fanfare in an unrelated key. Another silence, followed by music from yet a third musical world, a chorale tune in the brass. These three elements are like random musical boulders set alongside one another by the hand or mind of a crazy compositional imagination. No symphony had ever opened like this before.

The conductor and Brucknerphile John Butt has described this music as more like Igor Stravinsky's musical cubism than anything else in the nineteenth century, and in terms of the strangeness of the non-sequiturs in that sequence of three blocks of sound, he's right. The opening of this piece is more like Stravinsky's *Symphonies of Wind Instruments* than it is a memory of Beethoven's Ninth. The rest of the Fifth Symphony is a journey towards creating coherence and connection where, at the start, there is only incoherence and separation.

You want another weird symphonic opening? You got it: Bruckner's Sixth is supposedly in A major, but it opens with a dissonant meeting of major and minor keys. And again, there's no cosmic tremolo, but rather an obsessive musical Morse code in the upper strings, under which the cellos and basses play a snaking, chromatic tune. Where the Fifth and its opening is all about putting blocks of radically unconnected sounds and ideas next to one another, the Sixth is about layering them in ever more complex rhythmic pile-ups: two symphonies written one after the other, and two more gigantically opposed openings you couldn't imagine.

There are many other Bruckner clichés – that his symphonies are 'cathedrals of sound', that his music is on a monumental scale rather than a human one, that his music doesn't smile or dance – and none of them is true either. In fact, Bruckner is a time-travelling relativist, a feet-on-the-ground and spirit-in-the-sky human being and musician; a composer of terrible dances, as his youthful catalogue reveals – and utterly distinctive symphonies. So get your mind and your body, your ears and your feelings, around his symphonies; journey deeper into his world, and cross the threshold to another one.

Anton Bruckner

- ◀ *Lancier-Quadrilles* for piano
- ◀ *Aequali* for three trombones
- ◀ Symphony no. 5 in B flat major, first movement
- ◀ Symphony no. 6 in A major, first movement
- ◀ Symphony no. 8 in C minor, finale

Tchaikovsky's *Nutcracker*: strange enchantments

In theatreland at Christmas time, there's really only one story that families want to see: *Nutcracker* here, *Nutcracker* there, Tchaikovsky – everywhere! What's the secret of *The Nutcracker*'s success – as ballet, as score, as Christmas-conquering cultural and commercial phenomenon? Is everything really sweetness and light in its balletic world of sugar-plummed saccharinity? Or are there darknesses out there in the Land of Sweets, where Clara and her Prince are transported and where we in the audience are spirited in the second act of the story?

The Nutcracker's success was by no means the shoo-in it now seems to be. At its premiere in 1892, as part of a unique double-bill with Tchaikovsky's one-act opera *Iolanta*, the piece wasn't the runaway success that it is now. And that story is much stranger, and less innocent, than it at first seems. In the original *Nutcracker*, written in 1816 by E. T. A. Hoffmann, there are symbols and archetypes that point to an inherent darkness and symbolical strangeness in the ballet's drama.

That image of a mysterious Godfather leading the children, and Clara in particular, to a world beyond this one, taking her from childhood to adulthood, is ambiguously creepy, both as a story, and in the soundworld that Tchaikovsky's score creates.

The colonialist othering of the images of world cultures once we get to the Land of Sweets is there in Tchaikovsky's music in the naivety of the Orientalist caricatures, of his melodies and rhythms in the Arabian and Chinese Dances. You can see that stereotyping mirrored in the action on stage in the *chinoiserie* of the choreography at the Mariinsky Theatre in St Petersburg; or on film, in the way the mushrooms dance with Chinese hats in Disney's *Fantasia*.

But Tchaikovsky's score creates other, deeper and more meaningful currents under its exotic surfaces. In the music Tchaikovsky writes as a transition from this world to another, as the Christmas tree becomes a portal to another dimension, he creates a magical power that goes far beyond the needs of the narrative, with shimmering strings and voluptuously dangerous harmonies.

There are deep personal reasons, dramatically and bio-graphically, for the depth of the score of *The Nutcracker*. In the story of Clara's transformation, there's an echo of Tchaikovsky's perennial identification with the outsider. His sexuality is sub-limated into this story, and the character of Clara becomes a surrogate for his imagining of a place of perfected expression and indulgence, in which dreams become real, and in which the rules and conventions of the everyday are upended and suspended in a snow-globe fantasy of sugar plums and waltz-ing flowers. Tchaikovsky – like all of us when we see *The Nut-cracker* – wants to journey to that Land of Sweets. It's a vision of a world beyond this one that we want to inhabit, and from which we only reluctantly return. Don't we all wish we didn't have to come back to real life, but could stay in that fantastical fairyland of Tchaikovsky's music for ever? A dangerous bar-gain, maybe – but a seductive one: listen, and dance; let's go to the ball of the flowers and the frosts together . . .

Pyotr Ilyich Tchaikovsky: *The Nutcracker*

- ◀ 'Waltz of the Flowers'
- ◀ 'Dance of the Sugar Plum Fairy'
- ◀ *'Pas de deux'*
- ◀ 'Departure of the Guests'
- ◀ Tchaikovsky arr. Duke Ellington/Billy Strayhorn: *The Nutcracker Suite*

New World symphonies

16 December 1893, Carnegie Hall, New York. Antonín Dvořák's Ninth Symphony, 'From the New World', is about to have its premiere. As director of the non-segregated National Conservatory of Music, Dvořák is a man on a mission: thousands of miles from his native Bohemia, he has been tasked to lead American musical culture on the cusp of a new century. His inspiration isn't the Europe he left behind, but the sounds and songs of the America he encountered, from which he hopes to construct a new national music. 'The future music of this country must be founded', he writes, 'upon what are called the Negro melodies' – music he knew thanks to his black students, especially the songs sung by his assistant Harry T. Burleigh. 'Undoubtedly the germs for the best of music lie hidden among all the races that are comingled in this great country.'

At the thunderously successful New York Philharmonic premiere of the 'New World', Dvořák was sitting next to one of his favourite African American students, Maurice Arnold Strothotte, whose own symphony remains unpublished to this day. And while Dvořák's symphony has been turned into a spiritual – the melody sung by the cor anglais at the start of the slow movement became 'Goin' Home' in William Arms

Fisher's arrangement – and is played thousands of times every year by orchestras all over the world, it's as if Dvořák's real ambition never materialised. He didn't want his symphony to be *the* 'New World' Symphony, he wanted it to inspire generations of American composers, and especially African American composers, to write the true symphonies of the New World.

And they did. Yet the symphonies composed by black composers in America in the early decades of the twentieth century, often hugely successful with orchestras and audiences, have fallen victim to historical blindness and institutional prejudice, which means that some of the most important voices and pieces of American music just aren't performed enough in orchestral concerts. That must change – and you can start by hearing them yourself: symphonies by Florence Price, William Dawson and William Grant Still. Price's First Symphony, the first by an African American woman, is one of the most historically pioneering pieces of orchestral music, composed in 1932; Still's Symphony no. 1 'Afro-American', premiered in 1931, uses blues and swing – sounds that nobody had heard in a symphony before. And Dawson's *Negro Folk Symphony* is an essential piece, in which spirituals become thrillingly symphonic; its achievement is vital to understanding twentieth-century music.

◀ Antonín Dvořák: Symphony no. 9 in E minor, 'From the New World'
◀ Harry T. Burleigh: *Deep River*
◀ Florence Price: Symphony no. 1 in E minor
◀ William Grant Still: Symphony no. 1 in A flat major, 'Afro-American'
◀ William Dawson: *Negro Folk Symphony*

Gustav Mahler

Gustav Mahler's music is in the life-blood of concert halls all over the world. But Mahler remains misunderstood. So here's a case for Mahler as an anti-classical composer and ongoing musical radical, whose music shouldn't shore up the subscription seasons of orchestras and concert halls, but should rather be allowed to destabilise classical music culture from within.

Mahler's music comes from the street, the parade-ground and the mountainside, as much as it does from the traditions of Bach, Beethoven or Wagner. That's obvious as early as his First Symphony, that hymn to the Pan-ic power of the natural world, and to humanity's place within it. The third movement is still shocking. A solo double bass plays the tune, the nursery rhyme 'Frère Jacques' in a minor key, over a muffled timpani tattoo: music inspired by an image of an ironic funeral procession for a hunter, with the animals joyfully carrying his coffin. As Mahler said: 'The funeral march . . . one has to imagine as being played in a dull manner by a band of very bad musicians, as they usually follow such processions.' What's this music doing in a symphony? That confusion is just the start: Mahler also includes gypsy-bands that sound like klezmer groups, and songs from his youth, all in this one movement of the First Symphony. None of it is made from conventional 'classical music'.

Mahler suffuses each of his symphonies with the sounds of the real world. He was sampling sounds a century before popular music caught up with him. He includes military marches and off-stage soloists playing folk melodies in the Third Symphony; there are cowbells in the Sixth Symphony, designed to sound like the pastoral pealing of bovine lowing from a far-off pasture; there are heaven-storming choruses in the Second and Eighth Symphonies.

And yet Mahler's music plunges deeply inward too: in 'Der Abschied' ('The Farewell'), the final movement of his song-symphony, *Das Lied von der Erde* ('The Song of the Earth'), he creates a half-hour song for solo mezzo-soprano and orchestra. This is music that takes place on the edges of this world and the next, simultaneously taking leave of earthly existence and desperately hanging on to it, in ever quieter, more radiant, and more precious tendrils of sound – harp, celeste, the final sigh of the voice. The final notes of 'Der Abschied' are 'printed on the atmosphere', the composer Benjamin Britten once said.

Mahler – who was also an incendiarily inspiring conductor – once said to his fellow composer Jean Sibelius, when they met in Helsinki in 1907, that 'the symphony must be like the world – it must be all-embracing'. That's why Mahler's symphonies can't be contained by classical music culture. The sound stages and the imaginative spaces of his symphonies are all about the rest of the world – and, in 'Der Abschied', sounds that seem to come from beyond our world – rushing in to claim the concert hall. That's why we need them. They are forever contemporary, and forever radical.

Gustav Mahler

◀   Symphony no. 1: third movement
◀   Symphony no. 2: first movement
◀   Symphony no. 3: third movement
◀   Symphony no. 6: first movement
◀   Symphony no. 7: fourth movement

93

Debussy the impressionist?

Claude Debussy: musical impressionist, purveyor of sonic atmospherics and limpid, languid washes of sound.

Rubbish. Here's what Debussy himself said about that label, borrowed from the visual arts:

> I am trying to do 'something different' – an effect of reality . . . what the imbeciles call 'impressionism', a term which is as poorly used as possible, particularly by the critics, since they do not hesitate to apply it to [J. M. W.] Turner, the finest creator of mysterious effects in all the world of art.

If we only experience it properly, we'll hear how Debussy's music too is in search not of an insipid impression of the world, but of a new musical reality. Take one of his most famous orchestral pieces, *La Mer* ('The Sea'). Another clue to his essential creative project comes in what he says about Beethoven's 'Pastoral' Symphony – like *La Mer*, a piece inspired by the viscerality of nature. Debussy sees in Beethoven someone whose music transcended the picturesque, and became a force of symphonic nature, because parts of the 'Pastoral' achieve an 'expression more profound than the beauty of a landscape'. So when he's writing *La Mer*, between 1902 and 1905, Debussy is looking for that same spirit of transcendence, of music becoming an experience in its own right, independent of the images of the sea that might have inspired it.

And that's exactly what he does. *La Mer* is an alchemical combination of the materials of Debussy's art – its harmonies, its structures, its combinations of instruments – to produce new feelings for us in the audience. That's what happens throughout the third movement, the 'Dialogue between the wind and the sea'. A dialogue? More like a storm. It starts with timpani, bass drum, a low gong and the cellos and double basses, sounds made from the raw materials of the wind: white noise, ominous rumbles; a quake of sound answered by an avian keening in the woodwind.

But it's not the onomatopoeia of the music that counts, but the way Debussy's music generates its own discourse, its own 'effects of reality'. And the reality this music describes is pitiless and frightening. What's terrifying about it is that its uncanny swells and surges are wielded by the composer – there's nothing so predictable or natural as a wave or a gust of wind in *La Mer*, but rather music that obeys its own logic, that makes its own rules. This is a musical storm, not a maritime one, and that's why it opens up new kinds of feeling for us when we hear it.

La Mer ends with an ever-increasing maelstrom – a whirlpool made not by depicting nature, but by transcending it. Debussy piles his rhythms on top of one another to create a tsunami of friction and brutality. The end is a gasp of awe, as if the orchestra can no longer take the energy that Debussy has built up.

Claude Debussy: impressionist? Far from it. *La Mer* reveals him as a violent unleasher of new musical realities.

273

Claude Debussy

- ◀ 'Clair de lune', from *Suite bergamasque* for solo piano
- ◀ *La Mer*: third movement, 'Dialogue du vent et de la mer'
- ◀ *Jeux*, ballet score for orchestra
- ◀ *Pelléas and Mélisande*, Act 3, scene 2, 'Les souterrains du château'
- ◀ *Études* for piano: no. 3, 'Pour les quartes'

94

Maurice Ravel

What does beauty in music mean? If I say that the French composer Maurice Ravel's *Mother Goose* suite is 'beautiful', it's an almost meaningless cliché: beautiful sounds to accompany your rapturous reverie and to make you forget about the world outside, and other such hackneyed epithets. If Ravel's music is only beautiful, if that's its only aspiration, that's tantamount to saying that it's superficial, that it's all about the beauty of its surfaces rather than some mysterious depths that truly powerful music is supposed to have. But isn't beauty enough? What if beauty and its pursuit were Ravel's lifelong goals? And what if – shockingly, devastatingly – he achieved them?

Ravel was once accused of pretentiously playing the part of an aesthete, with his dandyish concern for every detail of how he dressed his small figure, as if he was denatured, putting on airs and graces rather than being in tune with reality. In response, Ravel said: 'But doesn't it ever occur to those people that I might be "artificial" by nature?'

Artificial by nature: Ravel was fully himself in exactly that way, right from the start of his composing career until the end, from the dreamily rococo *Menuet antique* from 1895, to the jazz- and blues-inspired G major Piano Concerto, composed in 1929–31: artificial – yet full of life.

The *lever du jour*, the sunrise, from his longest piece for orchestra, his ballet *Daphnis and Chloë*, proves the point of the beautiful artifices of Ravel's music. The scene starts with 'no sound – apart from the murmuring of tiny rivers of dew that have collected in the rocks', according to Michel Fokine's dramaturgy. Ravel's dewy murmuring is both deep and dazzling: it's made from glissandos in two harps and muted strings playing luminous harmonics, over a languidly sighing bass-line. In the woodwinds, there's what seems like a glittering wash of sound, but which is actually made of virtuosically precise patterns of twelve demisemiquavers. Ravel's musical birds, solo violins and a piccolo, join the scene, along with a wordless choir, glockenspiel and celeste: the music builds to three peaks of volume and intensity in a series of ever more sensuous climaxes.

Yet this music doesn't describe a sunrise at all. It's more powerful, and more beautiful, than any impression of nature. This music hasn't really got anything to do with that life-giving ball of nuclear fusion ninety-three million miles away. As Ravel's meticulousness shows in every bar of the score – all of those demisemiquavers that pass in a heartbeat but which are made with atomic-level musical exactitude – this is no natural phenomenon but an object of exquisite musical manufacture: artificial, unnatural. This isn't a sunrise, but something much rarer – an orchestra-rise.

Beauty is always a double-edged sword. On the dark side of the surface of the beautiful is death: the fading of momentary beauty into decay, rot, and the ravages of time. Yet when we're hearing Ravel's music, when we're overwhelmed by it, we're given an experience of a beauty that does not fade. Ravel's beauteous realm has its own rules outside the world, outside mortality. His music is an enchanted garden in which it is always beautiful – always Ravel.

Maurice Ravel

◀ 'The Fairy Garden', from *Mother Goose* suite
◀ *L'Enfant et les sortilèges*, opera in one act
◀ *Daphnis and Chloë*
◀ *La Valse*
◀ 'Asie', from the song-cycle *Shéhérazade*

95

The Second Viennese School

How to listen to music that's made of air from other planets: the music of the composers of the Second Viennese School – Arnold Schoenberg, Anton Webern and Alban Berg. They are musicians who are often thought to embody a quasi-scientific exploration of music in the twentieth century, thanks to the development of Schoenberg's so-called 'serialism', his system of composition with twelve tones. But that's not at all true: in reality, these three composers are navigators of new dimensions of musical feeling and human experience.

In 1908, in his Second String Quartet, Schoenberg led his music out of the walled garden of conventional harmonic relationships – keys like C major or F sharp minor, harmonies and chords that related to a tonal and expressive journey away from and back to a home key – to a region of radical, ethereal suspension. In this piece, the atmosphere of mystic contemplation that the four string players create is crowned by a solo soprano, singing the words of the poet Stefan George: 'I feel the air from another planets.' Schoenberg's quartet makes the sounds of these new regions, in which newly emancipated harmonies embody the images of the poem: the voice sings of beings 'dissolved into tones that circle and weave . . . I feel as if above the furthest cloud, swimming in a sea of crystalline radiance.' Schoenberg's music, flying free of conventional tonality, comes from the expressive necessity of inhabiting the imagery of the poem.

Schoenberg wrote about the emotional urgency of his music to another visionary composer, Ferruccio Busoni:

> Harmony is expression and nothing else . . . it is impossible for a person to have only one sensation at a time. One has thousands simultaneously . . . And this variegation, this multifariousness, this illogicality which our senses demonstrate, set forth by some mounting rush of blood, by some reaction of the senses or the nerves, this I should like to have in my music.

That's an invitation not just to composers to find another way to write music, but to us as listeners to allow those thousands of sensations to be set free.

That's what the hyper-compressed scores of Anton Webern are all about, releasing emotions that are both volcanic and crystalline in music like his Six Bagatelles for String Quartet or his Orchestral Pieces, op. 10; there's the teeming world of vertiginous emotion of Alban Berg's Three Orchestral Pieces, and the sheer expressive tumult that Schoenberg created in music like his Five Orchestral Pieces and his operatic psycho-drama for soprano and orchestra, *Erwartung*.

All this music releases a Pandora's box of pure feeling, in which there seems no difference and no distance between the extreme emotions and experiences these composers are communicating and their embodiment in sound. If it's challenging to hear, it's only because this music mirrors the churning dynamism of our own emotional lives, reflecting our fears and darknesses, as well as our ecstasies and pleasures.

Which is why Schoenberg's later development of his method of 'composition with twelve tones' was simply a way to try and rationalise the regions of emancipated feeling that he and Berg and Webern had discovered. Forget the image of desiccated dissonance, and throw yourself into the maelstrom of fearlessly expressive intensity that all three composers create.

◀ Alban Berg: *Wozzeck*, Act 1, scene 3
◀ Alban Berg: Three Pieces for Orchestra, op. 6
◀ Arnold Schoenberg: String Quartet no. 2, fourth movement
◀ Arnold Schoenberg: Six Little Piano Pieces, op. 19
◀ Anton Webern: no. 4 from Five Pieces for Orchestra, op. 10

96

Rewilding Sibelius

The finale of the Finnish composer Jean Sibelius's Fifth Symphony is famously inspired by a natural phenomenon, when Sibelius saw a flight of precisely sixteen swans across the lake from his house, north of Helsinki: 'one of my greatest experiences. Lord God, that Beauty.' He composed a swinging tune in the horns, and another declamatory melody above them. And repeated enough, that way of thinking about this music calcifies into truth, so that the tunes and the swans weld together in our imagination, as if the music were a depiction of their flight, and a reflection of the awed gaze of the composer – or of any of us, faced with that natural spectacle, those huge birds taking wing, improbably, beating and thudding the air.

But the experience of Sibelius's music in this piece is much more elemental than reflecting a gaze at the natural world. Sibelius's music isn't really a depiction of swans in flight, it isn't a prettified version of the wilderness of forest and lake and snow and light. It's music as its own wildness, a symphonic force of nature in its own right.

The wild places of Sibelius's music are experiences in sound that return us to primal feelings: of being lost, as we are in the middle of the first movement of the Fifth Symphony, when we find ourselves in an unnavigable forest of harmonically

281

unstable musical briars that tangle around our listening consciousness. Or his music transforms and breaks apart the orchestra with the visceral power of a pagan creation myth, as in the tone-poem *Luonnotar*.

But the wildest and most 'self-willed' music Sibelius ever wrote (echoing the writer Jay Griffiths's description of wilderness as 'self-willed' landscapes) is his last tone-poem, *Tapiola*, composed in 1926. The entire piece is based on just one melody, a musical bacterium that proliferates and spreads through *Tapiola*'s eighteen minutes. Its final climax is the wildest moment of all. A swarm billows into a blizzard of blinding semitonal obsessions in the strings, and there's nothing we can do to stop this musically self-willed stormscape, until we're the teeth of the typhoon: there are soul-searing screams in the brass, the sounds of the primeval world reaching across to ours, cutting through across the aeons to find us wherever we're listening – wildness calling to wildness. *Tapiola* isn't a depiction of anything in nature, it's a self-willed musical supernature.

The breath of the wild in Sibelius's music is an urgent call to our primal natures. If we really hear it, we'll find an echo of experiences that we need more than ever: of being lost, of being infinitesimal, experiencing forces that we can't control as our listening is entangled with cycles of time that are more powerful than we can possibly know.

Jean Sibelius

◀ *Luonnotar* for soprano and orchestra
◀ *Tapiola*
◀ Symphony no. 5, finale
◀ Symphony no. 7
◀ *The Oceanides*

97

Igor Stravinsky: Understood best by Children and Animals

Will the real Igor Stravinsky please stand up? Is he the composer who tore the musical earth apart with his ballet *The Rite of Spring* in 1913, a piece that sent shockwaves that composers are still recovering from? Maybe: but then Stravinsky is also the composer of acerbically modernist, dissonantly chic 1950s serialism, music like *Movements* for piano and orchestra – a piece that was utterly unexpected from the composer who had also created the neoclassical consonant cool of the ballet *Orpheus*, from the late 1940s. Then there's the Stravinsky who wrote geometric jazz for Benny Goodman in the *Ebony Concerto*, and the much younger composer who produced late-Romantic Russian colourism in his Symphony in E flat.

He's five different composers in those five different pieces, composed in three countries, from Russia to France to America – and I could go on, creating an ever more discombobulating musical montage of music from nearly seventy years of a compositional career. Did Stravinsky jump from style to style like a musical magpie, searching out the latest trend and newest fad to define, describe and discard, before moving on to the next one? Is there a stable something underneath it all: an identity, a way of hearing, a way of understanding, an essential tincture of experience and approach that we can call Stravinskian?

I think it's this. Stravinsky's music is proof of one of the deepest truths that art has: that we draw closer to the thing we are hearing or observing not by copying it or claiming it, but by remaking it. That's why Stravinsky turns all the multiple musical pasts that his work is based on – folk musics, early opera, ancient Greek myths, or twentieth-century musical styles like serialism – into an ever-resonant present tense. And in that gap, in that creative distance, in that exile, he remakes the world, and turns the music around him into these new forms and shapes and experiences. Stravinsky allows us to see and to hear things for what they really are.

Which is why – as well as his innovations in rhythm, texture, music theatre, and harmony – Stravinsky still feels like a contemporary composer. His music is still the most complete answer to the question of what you do when you feel everything has been done already, the situation that today's composers find themselves in, even more acutely. How do you become more yourself as a composer, the more music you hear and filter through your creative prism? From Anthony Braxton to John Zorn, from Judith Weir to Thomas Adès, from Elliott Carter to Steve Reich – the way they have all differently dealt with Stravinsky is at the core of their creativity. As Adès has said, in *Full of Noises*, a book of interviews from 2012: 'For a composer, Stravinsky is like a terminus you have to go through to get anywhere.'

Igor Stravinsky

◀ *The Rite of Spring*
◀ *Movements* for piano and orchestra
◀ *Pulcinella*
◀ *Oedipus Rex*
◀ *Variations: Aldous Huxley in memoriam*

98

Shostakovich's Symphony no. 15

On 14 August 1975, the violinist Mark Lubotsky was among the mourners in the Great Hall of the Moscow Conservatoire for the composer Dmitri Shostakovich's funeral. He described his encounter with Shostakovich's body:

> It all seems somewhat strange . . . The coffin is in the hall. A black pedestal with three steps at right angles to the platform. Shostakovich. Too much pinkish-red make-up. Unrecognisable. Except for his arms. Unnaturally small from shoulders to wrists, and the hands dead and waxy, but his own, in some terrible way his own.

That image of Shostakovich's body is chilling, grotesque, even morbidly comic; the idea of his body and his mortal remains turned into something 'unrecognisable', uncanny, not quite his own – yet nobody else's, of course.

Four years earlier, in 1971, Shostakovich composed his last symphony, the Fifteenth. And this symphony too is uncanny, zombified: his own, and not his own. It's a piece made from a tissue of his own musical past and tattered fragments, shards, and memories of music by composers from Rossini to Wagner to Mahler to Glinka to Rachmaninoff, as well as Shostakovich's fourteen-strong symphonic pre-history.

The most obvious quotation is from Rossini's *William Tell* Overture. It suddenly but softly bursts through the music a couple of minutes into the first movement of the Fifteenth Symphony. What is this over-familiar operatic earworm doing in the first movement of Shostakovich's last symphony? From the other end of the expressive universe, what do the lugubrious quotations from Wagner's *Ring* cycle mean in the final movement of the Fifteenth? These quotations, like a classical-music precursor of sampling, are unmoored from their original world of reference and meaning, so that they're alien interlopers that are yet made part of the weird warp and weft of Shostakovich's symphony in 1971. Shostakovich himself told his friend Isaak Glikman, when he asked him about the quotations: 'I don't myself quite know why the quotations are there, but I could not, could not, not include them' – a typically tortuous bit of triple-negativity.

Riddles and enigmas. Mind you, Shostakovich's own music is weird enough on its own terms. The symphony starts with a glockenspiel and a solo flute, the glockenspiel sounding like the chime of a door you walk through into a favourite toyshop. Shostakovich said that the first movement was a vision of a toy emporium – but as it develops, with its frightening explosions and jump-cuts, it's more like a toy grenade that goes off in a child's hands, blowing the symphony apart from the inside. The Soviet Union's most famous toyshop was just opposite the Lubyanka in Moscow, the headquarters of the KGB. Play could have serious consequences in the Soviet regime.

The symphony ends in its fourth movement with an utterly empty string accompaniment of an A major chord, over which the percussionists return to the clockwork mechanisms of the screwed-up toyshop, winding itself down. What does Shostakovich's Fifteenth Symphony mean? Everything – in the endless ways it can be interpreted and in the play between the quotations and Shostakovich's own multiple musical voices – and, in the profoundest and bravest sense – nothing. This music gives us the nihilising experience of facing the most disturbing yet essential truth we can imagine: that our lives are no more meaningful than the striking of a little bell to begin, and another to end.

◀ Dmitri Shostakovich: Symphony no. 15 in A major
◀ Dmitri Shostakovich: Symphony no. 7 in C major, 'Leningrad'
◀ Dmitri Shostakovich: String Quartet no. 13 in B flat minor
◀ Alfred Schnittke: *Suite in the Old Style*
◀ Nas: *Hip Hop Is Dead*

Deep Listening: Pauline Oliveros

What is deep listening? . . .
Take a walk at night. Walk so silently that the bottoms of
your feet become ears . . .

This is listening not just as an activity, but as a way of being,
and a way of creating. It's a Sonic Meditation by the American
composer, improviser, accordionist, electronic artist, and cre-
ator of whole oceans of sound, Pauline Oliveros, who died at
the end of 2016 at the age of eighty-four. It's not just that Deep
Listening is Oliveros's idea: it's her album, it's her band, it's her
philosophy, and it's even her copyrighted trademark.

But Deep Listening is also something that belongs to all
of us. Becoming a deep listener means opening up a world of
sound, all the time, through the delight of paying attention to
the sounds of our environments – urban and rural, natural and
man-made. Be warned – you may just find that to listen deeply
to the world is to have it changed forever.

There's a very specific moment in 1989, where Deep Listening as practice, and as pretty terrible pun, really gets cemented
as an idea in Pauline Oliveros's life and music-making, thanks
to a disused military cistern fourteen feet under the ground
of an otherwise unremarkable bit of country in America's

Washington State, where she recorded the first album with her Deep Listening Band, along with the trombonist Stuart Dempster and the vocalist Panaiotis. They were underground, after all, so the name stuck, and the music they made in the echoes of the gigantic reverberation time of the chamber is a hypnotically vast feedback loop, an awesomely resonating halo of sound.

But Oliveros's life as a deep listener began much earlier than that. It began even before her birth in 1932, even if she didn't realise it: one of the most gently powerful things I heard her say was that our sense of hearing is the first to develop in the womb, and the last to leave us when we die. Which means that our deaths pass in an echo of our own listening. Deep Listening spans our whole lives.

Here's another of Oliveros's Sonic Meditations:

As you listen, the particles of sound (phonons) decide to be heard. Listening affects what is sounding. The relationship is symbiotic.
As you listen, the environment is enlivened.
This is the listening effect.

It's not just that we're listening to the environment, we're changing it – enlivening it, quickening it into a different kind of existence – through our listening. As Pauline Oliveros knew, and as her music and her Deep Listening project proves, listening really can change the world.

Pauline Oliveros

◀ 'Bye Bye Butterfly'
◀ 'To Valerie Solanas and Marilyn Monroe in Recognition
    of Their Desperation'
◀ Deep Listening Band: 'Lear'
◀ Deep Listening Band: 'Johina'
◀ Pauline Oliveros with Ione: 'Water Above Sky
    Below Now'

100

Kaija Saariaho

What are your dreams like? Are they flashes of light that irradiate your imagination, or are they full of cosseting twilight, or surreally twisted natural forms, shapes – and sounds? And when you wake up, don't you long to return to that delicious, dazzling dream state?

The Finnish composer Kaija Saariaho manages to do exactly that: her works are dream-worlds that that the rest of us can access in our waking lives. Saariaho's music dares to venture across the veil that usually separates our dream visions from our daily lives. Her music is a passport to worlds of cosmic luminosity, like her orchestral piece *Orion*, from 2002, which turns the musicians into celestial travellers. She has composed a flute concerto that makes birds dance in the galaxy – *Aile du songe*, from 2001; she has made pieces that fuse crystalline hardness with the evanescence of smoke, vapours and scents, in *Du Cristal* . . . and . . . *À la Fumée*, composed in 1989 and 1990; and she has crossed sonic borders between electronic surrealism and acoustic reality in *Verblendungen*, written in 1984. And in her operas Kaija Saariaho journeys to the inside of the deepest emotions that we can experience in our lives: love and loss, longing and grief, all turned into an ecstatic outpouring of musical feeling in *L'Amour de loin* ('Love from afar'), written at the turn of the millennium.

Saariaho's dream worlds began in her early years. Born in Finland in 1952, she had no music in her family life – yet her world was filled with musical sounds. It's just that she didn't know where they were coming from. As a young child, she remembers that she would hear music throughout the day, and especially vividly at night. There was a radio in the house – but that wasn't the explanation.

I also heard music when I was a girl that didn't come from a radio. It was music that was in my mind. I imagined that it came from my pillow. My mother remembered me asking her to turn the pillow off at night when I couldn't sleep, to turn off the music that I imagined inside my head.

Dreaming in music: in her adult musical life, from the electronic studios of IRCAM in Paris to the world's opera houses, Saariaho has made her creative mission an exploration of these inner worlds of imagination, mapping these fundamentally private regions of experience into musical worlds that we can all share.

Kaija Saariaho's music isn't unique only because of her contribution to fusing electronics with live musicians, or her visionary orchestral music, or her six full-length operas. It's because in sounding out that border between dream and waking, she has alchemised a fundamental power that music always has, but which has rarely been revealed so magically or so consistently by any composer. Listen to her music and be transported into a shared dream-world.

Kaija Saariaho

- ◀ *L'Amour de loin*, opera
- ◀ *Orion*, for orchestra
- ◀ *Petals*, for cello and electronics
- ◀ *Lichtbogen*, for nine instruments and live electronics
- ◀ *Du Cristal* . . . and . . . *à la Fumée*, for alto flute, cello, electronics and orchestra

101

Wagner's *Ring* cycle

A woman makes the world end. What does she see? What does she hear? Apocalypse, destruction, purification by fire and water, a maelstrom of the music we've been listening to for the last four days – Brünnhilde brings about the end of the gods and ushers in a new world at the very end of Richard Wagner's *Ring* cycle.

Why does the world of the *Ring* cycle come to this? A project that took a quarter of a century to create for Wagner, its composer, dramatist and poet; and which takes four music dramas and four nights for us to experience: why does it end with this musical apocalypse at the end of *Götterdämmerung* ('Twilight of the Gods'), the final music drama in the *Ring*?

Wagner said that the entire story of the *Ring* exists to show how 'a woman becomes wise' through 'love's profoundest suffering'. And at the end of the story, Brünnhilde, the Valkyrie who gave up her immortality in the name of love, throws herself on Siegfried's funeral pyre and brings about the destruction of Valhalla: the realm of her father, the self-annihilating god Wotan. And the Ring – the symbol of the accursed power that corrupts everyone who touches it throughout all four music dramas – returns to the water with the Rhinemaidens.

What does it all mean? For all of the ideas about the *Ring* – its tangled web of philosophy, musical revolution, social change and mythic experience – there's a strain of thought that it all means precisely nothing; that it's an essay in nihilism, a mish-mash of Nordic myth fused with the cosmology of Wagner's own ego, a confused mess of proto-socialist and proto-fascist ideas, so that its drama is a gigantic exercise in futility. What was the point of all that? To end up in the Rhine, in the same place with much of the same music you started out with, all those hours and days ago?

There are clues in the embers of the apocalypse of the end of the cycle, because for all the immolation and fiery destruction, the stage isn't empty. In fact, what's left is a crowd of men and women. The gods and dwarves have been extinguished, but human beings remain. Wagner says in his stage directions that 'the men and women' of the Rhine 'surge into the foreground as far as is possible' . . . 'extremely moved, [they] watch the growing glow of fire in the sky.' In Patrice Chéreau's centenary production of the *Ring* cycle at Wagner's theatre in Bayreuth in 1976, a crowd of men, women and children turned towards the audience at the very end of *Götterdämmerung*, as if asking the question: the world now belongs to us – so what are we going to do with it? The gods have failed, will we do better than Wotan and Alberich, than Brünnhilde and Siegfried?

Will we accept Wagner's challenge? That challenge is – change. The four dramas of the *Ring* are an object lesson in how not to make a world, as all of the efforts of the gods, humans and monsters end in catastrophe. After those sixteen hours and four days, we aren't really back where we began: we're much, much further back than that. After this mythic revelation of the limits of power and the limitlessness of love, we're faced with a primordial decision in the aftershock of the cathartic tumult of the music at the end of *Götterdämmerung*. On the cliff-edge at the end of the *Ring* cycle, we all need to decide: what world shall we make now?

◀ Richard Wagner: 'Brünnhilde's Immolation', from
   Götterdämmerung
◀ Richard Wagner: Prelude, from *Das Rheingold*
◀ Richard Wagner: 'The Ride of the Valkyries', from
   Die Walküre
◀ Rick Wakeman: 'The Inferno Ride', from Ken Russell's
   film *Lisztomania*
◀ Anna Russell: *The Ring of the Nibelungs – An Analysis*

Acknowledgements

This book is indebted to everyone at BBC Radio 3 who created *The Listening Service* in 2016, especially the Controller, Alan Davey, Edward Blakeman, and Jessica Isaacs, who had the vision to turn the show into a reality, and who commissioned Radio 3's teams to produce it.

And it's Radio 3's brilliant producers to whom the book is dedicated. Their genius in turning the words that each programme starts with into the unique mix of music and speech that defines the sound of *The Listening Service* is an ever-humbling revelation of what's possible when the most creative people are allowed the freedom to make a new kind of radio, and when they give themselves to the subjects that mean the most to them.

The Listening Service is a collaboration, a meeting of minds and ideas and energy that, we all hope, communicates just as excitingly to our audiences as it's a thrill for us to make. Being part of the programme, writing and delivering the scripts, is the most fulfilling role I could imagine in radio, because of the privilege of working with these astoundingly inspirational people, whose names should be in the title of every programme they make, and whose friendship is the essential crucible that makes the show work.

So thank you, in radiophonic excelsis, to Elizabeth Funning, for leading the programme for its first five years, to Hannah Thorne, whose creativity catalysed the fundamental idea of the strand, and to all of the other producers who have given so much to every show they have made: David Papp, Philip Tagney, Georgia Mann, Ruth Thomson, Paul Frankl, Calantha Bonnissent, Graham Rogers, Juan Carlos Jaramillo, Jeremy Evans, and Elizabeth Arno; to the assistant producers who have worked on the programme, and to the show's editors, Edwina Wolstencroft and Sue Roberts.

This book couldn't have happened without Belinda Matthews's editorial vision at Faber, without Joanna Harwood's, Kate Hopkins's, and Michael Downes's forensic care over the text; and it wouldn't have been possible without the support of my agent, Kerry Glencorse, at Susanna Lea Associates.

Above all: this book, and all of the programmes, are made for you. Thank you for reading, and listening. And enjoy your further adventures, connecting musical cultures together, and being open to the whole world of music, that we all hope the book and the shows inspire.